BACK ON
TOP

THE PENGUINS INCREDIBLE RUN TO THEIR FOURTH STANLEY CUP CHAMPIONSHIP

Katherine Grigsby, Layout & Design

ISBN: 978-1-940056-42-5

Printed in the United States of America
KCI Sports Publishing   3340 Whiting Avenue, Suite 5   Stevens Point, WI 54481
Phone: 1-800-697-3756   Fax: 715-344-2668
www.kcisports.com

CONTENTS

Pittsburgh Penguins players celebrate after beating the San Jose Sharks in Game 6 of the NHL hockey Stanley Cup Finals. AP Photo

PITTSBURGH PENGUINS STANLEY CUP CHAMPIONS

Pittsburgh fans have waited seven long years to utter those words, and finally, the Penguins are back on top. Let the celebration begin!

It's been a long wait for Penguins Nation, but every card-carrying member will tell you it's been well worth it. This was a Cup victory that had been months in the making. Mike Sullivan had a clear vision for this Penguins team when he was hired as the new head coach in December: play to the strengths of Sidney Crosby, Phil Kessel, Kris Letang and the rest of the team's best players.

Mission accomplished.

The Penguins gritty, tough-as-nails approach of out-working, out-hitting and out-hustling its opponents was on full display throughout their run to the Cup. With the leadership of Crosby, the toughness of Letang and the goal-scoring prowess of Kessel this Pittsburgh team answered the bell at every turn. And where would this Penguins team be without the contributions of its unheralded rookies Conor Sheary, Matt Murray, Bryan Rust and Tom Kuhnhackl?

In the following pages, our staff proudly brings you on a trip down memory lane through the Penguins' playoff run that came to its jubilant conclusion in Game 6 against the San Jose Sharks. Use this keepsake as a compass, carrying you along the path of the champion Penguins. We provide you the best view in the house of all the ups and downs through the playoffs and give you an inside look at the incredible journey that brought Lord Stanley's Cup back to Pittsburgh.

Celebrate this season and save this book to revisit the Penguins' magical moments and the hard-working, hard-hitting and hard-to-forget players – both stars and role guys – who rewarded your faith in the Black 'n' Gold by climbing back to the top of the heap in the NHL.

Welcome back Penguins! Let's do it again soon.

KCI Sports Publishing

Penguins Patric Hornqvist
(72) celebrates his third
period goal. AP Photo

HORNQVIST HAT TRICK LIFTS PENGUINS PAST RANGERS

Penguins goalie Jeff Zatkoff (37) stops a shot as Phil Kessel (81) lifts the stick of New York Rangers Marc Staal (18) to keep him from the rebound. AP Photo

Banished to the third string in January, Jeff Zatkoff could have checked out. Instead, the Pittsburgh goalie kept showing up at the rink every day, cracking jokes to keep things loose and helping rookie Matt Murray -- who took Zatkoff's job as primary backup to Marc-Andre Fleury -- get used to life in the NHL.

Then a concussion sidelined Fleury. Ditto,

Murray. And suddenly Pittsburgh's forgotten man was thrust into the role of unlikely starter heading into the playoffs. Zatkoff hardly looked overcome by the stage. Steady at the start and sharp throughout, Zatkoff made 35 saves in the Penguins' 5-2 victory over the New York Rangers in Game 1 of the Eastern Conference quarterfinals.

"He was our best player," said Pittsburgh forward Patric Hornqvist after his first career playoff hat trick.

And every bit the equal of New York star Henrik Lundqvist, who played just 20 minutes before exiting after taking a stick to the eye from teammate Marc Staal late in the first period.

Staal was tied up in front of the New York net when his stick found its way in between the bars on Lundqvist's facemask. Lundqvist writhed in pain on the ice for several moments and stayed through the end of the period, the last shot he faced a rebound from Hornqvist that gave the Penguins a lead they would never relinquish.

Antti Raanta stepped in and was shaky, giving up three goals on 19 shots as Pittsburgh took advantage once Lundqvist -- who had won seven of his last eight playoff starts against the Penguins -- left. Derek Stepan scored twice but the Rangers saw their four-game road winning streak in Pittsburgh come to an abrupt halt.

"There were a few things I think we can build on, but I do know that we've got quite a few guys that need to play better than they did tonight," New York coach Alain Vigneault said. "We're going to have to play better as a team."

Sidney Crosby had a goal and two assists for Pittsburgh and rookie Tom Kuhnhackl also scored for the Penguins, but the star was the understated 28-year-old goalie who took his demotion in stride. He spent plenty of time with Pittsburgh goaltending coach Mike Bales to stay sharp. Tasked with keeping the 14-2 surge the Penguins put together to end the regular season

intact, Zatkoff went about his business with the crispness surprising for a player making just his sixth appearance since Jan. 1.

"You just have to make sure you're staying ready in case the team needs you and finding you times to get on the ice to get those shots and get that work," Zatkoff said. "Obviously not the circumstances you want to come in."

New York dominated the opening minutes, throwing shots at Zatkoff from all angles rather than trying to set anything up. Zatkoff lacks Fleury's athleticism but managed to scramble when required, keeping the Penguins afloat early while his teammates took time to find their legs.

"It's not an easy situation to come into," Crosby said. "We kind of had a slow start, they tested him a lot early and he made some big saves. Just a great game from him and allowed us to kind of get comfortable out there and get our game back."

"I'll enjoy it tonight," Zatkoff said. "But, you know, get focused on Game 2 and I just continue to work hard no matter what happens. You can't predict what's going to happen."

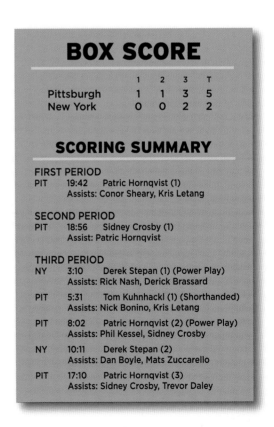

BOX SCORE

	1	2	3	T
Pittsburgh	1	1	3	5
New York	0	0	2	2

SCORING SUMMARY

FIRST PERIOD
PIT   19:42   Patric Hornqvist (1)
Assists: Conor Sheary, Kris Letang

SECOND PERIOD
PIT   18:56   Sidney Crosby (1)
Assist: Patric Hornqvist

THIRD PERIOD
NY   3:10   Derek Stepan (1) (Power Play)
Assists: Rick Nash, Derick Brassard

PIT   5:31   Tom Kuhnhackl (1) (Shorthanded)
Assists: Nick Bonino, Kris Letang

PIT   8:02   Patric Hornqvist (2) (Power Play)
Assists: Phil Kessel, Sidney Crosby

NY   10:11   Derek Stepan (2)
Assists: Dan Boyle, Mats Zuccarello

PIT   17:10   Patric Hornqvist (3)
Assists: Sidney Crosby, Trevor Daley

Penguins Patric Hornqvist (72) puts the puck behind Rangers goalie Antti Raanta (32) for his second goal of the game.
AP Photo

Penguins Evgeni Malkin (71) collides with New York Rangers Derick Brassard (16). AP Photo

LUNDQVIST RETURNS AS RANGERS EVEN SERIES

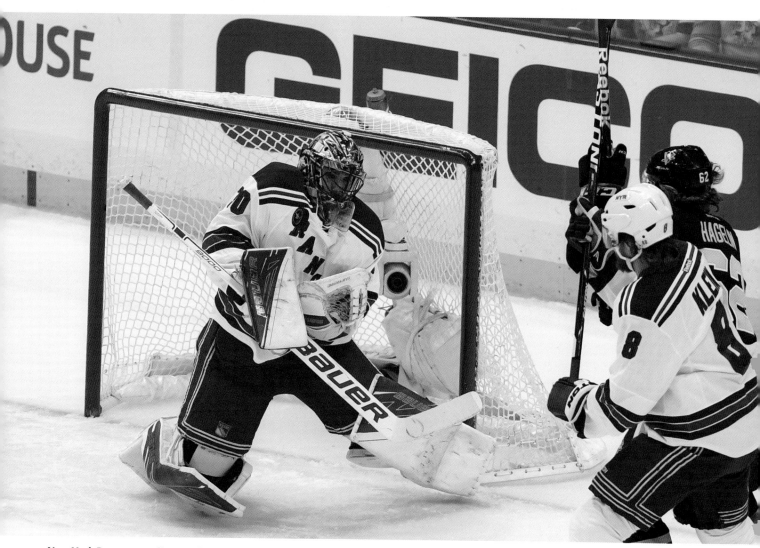

New York Rangers goalie Henrik Lundqvist (30) makes a save during the first period. AP Photo

Henrik Lundqvist's right eye is just fine, thanks.

So, too, are the New York Rangers, whose franchise goaltender is back to looking like the foundation for New York's near annual deep postseason run.

Three days removed from a freakish run-in between his face and teammate Marc Staal's stick, Lundqvist looked like his ever steady self, making 29 saves, and the Rangers took advantage of some sloppy defensive play by Pittsburgh in a 4-2 victory that evened their Eastern Conference

Penguins Phil Kessel (81) puts the puck past a sprawling New York Rangers goalie Henrik Lundqvist (30) for a second period goal. **AP Photo**

quarterfinal series at 1-1.

Lundqvist sat out the final two periods of a Game 1 setback after Staal's stick made its way through Lundqvist's cage, scraping his right eye.

Lundqvist saw a specialist on Thursday, practiced on Friday and spent three periods on Saturday doing what he always seems to do this time of year.

"When you know there's nothing wrong with the eye, you know you can just go out there and just push yourself and whatever is feeling uncomfortable, you don't really think about it when the game starts," Lundqvist said. "You just want to be out there and you're very determined."

Lundqvist kept the surging Penguins, boosted by the return of star center Evgeni Malkin, at bay for most of the first 30 minutes then saw his team pounce when Pittsburgh went through the kind of lull it largely avoided while ending the regular season with a 14-2 burst.

Keith Yandle and Derick Brassard scored 18 seconds apart in the second period to give the Rangers the lead, and Mats Zuccarello and Chris Kreider piled on later as New York improved to 6-2 since the start of the 2014 playoffs in the game immediately following a loss.

J.T. Miller added three assists as the Rangers handed Pittsburgh just its third loss since March 6.

Phil Kessel scored his first two playoff goals in three years. Backup goaltender Jeff Zatkoff made

Pittsburgh defenseman Olli Maatta couldn't handle a bouncing puck and Brassard raced by him to beat Zatkoff for Brassard's seventh goal in his past 10 playoff games against the Penguins.

Officials reviewed the goal to see if Brassard's feet crossed the blue line before the puck, but replays were inconclusive and the Rangers were ahead to stay.

"I guess I was fine," Brassard said.

A few minutes later, New York was better than that. Zuccarello's doubled the Rangers' advantage on a play that looked like a mirror image of Yandle's score, sneaking toward the far post behind Pittsburgh's defense and slamming a pass from Miller into the net 16:52 into the second.

When Trevor Daley's turnover along the goal line early in the third period offered Kreider an easy opportunity that he didn't miss, the Rangers were on their way to the kind of bounce-back performance that's become typical of their postseason resilience under coach Alain Vigneault.

Having Lundqvist at the back end to cover up mistakes certainly helps.

"Good feeling to go home now, and then we get an opportunity to play at home," Lundqvist said. "I can't wait."

24 stops while making a second consecutive start in place of injured Marc-Andre Fleury, but was undone by some shaky play in front of him.

"When our team is at its best, we've been defending really well," Pittsburgh coach Mike Sullivan said. "I think a couple of the goals were uncharacteristic of this group."

Pittsburgh led at the midway point on Kessel's power-play goal 3:21 into the second before the next 10 minutes changed the direction of the series.

Yandle tied it 12:38 into the second when Brassard won a faceoff in the left circle and Miller swooped in to get it before passing it to Yandle in the right circle. Brassard wasted little time giving the Rangers their first lead of the series when

BOX SCORE

	1	2	3	T
Pittsburgh	0	1	1	2
New York	0	3	1	4

SCORING SUMMARY

SECOND PERIOD

PIT   3:21   Phil Kessel (1) (Power Play)
Assists: Trevor Daley, Nick Bonino

NY   12:38   Keith Yandle (1)
Assists: Rick Nash, J.T. Miller

NY   12:56   Derick Brassard (1)
Assists: J.T. Miller, Brady Skjei

NY   16:52   Mats Zuccarello (1)
Assist: J.T. Miller

THIRD PERIOD

NY   0:39   Chris Kreider (1)
Assist: Derick Brassard

PIT   5:42   Phil Kessel (2) (Power Play)
Assists: Nick Bonino, Evgeni Malkin

Penguins Matt Cullen (7), Ben Lovejoy (12), and Bryan Rust (17) celebrate after Cullen scored the game-winning goal early in the third period.   AP Photo

EASTERN CONFERENCE

QUARTERFINALS APRIL 19, 2016 MADISON SQUARE GARDEN MANHATTAN, NEW YORK

PITTSBURGH PENGUINS 3 ● NEW YORK RANGERS 1

CULLEN'S LATE GOAL LEADS PENGUINS OVER RANGERS

Penguins defenseman Trevor Daley (6) looks to clear New York Rangers Derek Stepan (21) as Stepan attempts to block the view of goalie Matt Murray (30). **AP Photo**

The Pittsburgh Penguins got back to playing the style that made them one of the NHL's best teams after Christmas.

They played defense. They got goals from their stars, a game-winner from 39-year-old Matt Cullen and a solid effort from rookie goaltender Matt Murray.

They also got the benefit of a video review on

Penguins center Sidney Crosby (87) and teammate Patrick Hornqvist (72) celebrate after Crosby's power play goal. AP Photo

an offside call that saved them a goal in a 3-1 win in Game 3 of the first-round playoff series with the New York Rangers.

Even the return of Rangers captain Ryan McDonagh could not slow down the Penguins or prevent them from taking a 2-1 lead in their first-round playoff series.

"We understand if you want to win games, that's how you're going to have to win them this time of year," said Penguins star Sidney Crosby, whose power-play goal late in the second period tied the game at 1-all.

"Our mindset is playing the right way, doing the things that have got us here. The past is the past. Right now we want to make sure we are better every game. I think we took a good step here tonight."

The Penguins dominated this one, limiting the Rangers to 17 shots. Most were not very good and

time in the series. He was hurt in the final weekend of the regular season and Jeff Zatkoff started the first two games with Marc-Andre Fleury out with a concussion.

"The nerves were definitely going at the start of the game. That's understandable," Murray said. "It was my first playoff game, at MSG no less. I was able to control it and that was all I could ask for."

The Penguins made all the big plays after Nash scored. Crosby gave the team a lift scoring late in the second period and Cullen made the big play early in the third, beating Henrik Lundqvist (28 saves) on a semi-breakaway after beating two defensemen at 4:16.

Cullen's game-winner was as much a good play by him and a bad one by defensemen Keith Yandle and Dan Boyle.

Cullen took a pass and entered the Rangers zone. Yandle and Boyle converged on him and ran into each other.

"It was kind of a tough puck," Cullen said. "It was bouncing a lot tonight. That one just went to a perfect spot. I was in the right spot and was able to poke it by. I was just happy to see it go in."

Kris Letang added an empty-net goal to ice the game.

Crosby got his second goal of the series after Marc Staal took a hooking penalty with a minute left in the second period. The Penguins needed 18 seconds to convert, with Crosby redirecting Phil Kessel's attempt into the net from about two feet away.

Rangers did little after Rick Nash scored short-handed early in the second period.

"We kept saying it, we kept telling ourselves, we had to lay it in and shoot it," said McDonagh, who missed the first two games of the series with a upper-body (hand) injury.

"I'm sure we'll look at some things when we watch the game and wish we had put more pucks on the net especially because it was his (Murray's) first game in a while."

Murray was barely tested in playing for the first

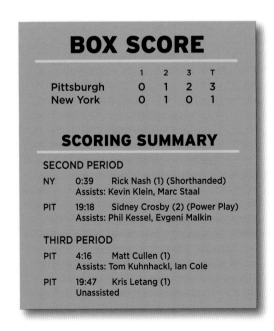

BOX SCORE

	1	2	3	T
Pittsburgh	0	1	2	3
New York	0	1	0	1

SCORING SUMMARY

SECOND PERIOD

NY	0:39	Rick Nash (1) (Shorthanded)
		Assists: Kevin Klein, Marc Staal
PIT	19:18	Sidney Crosby (2) (Power Play)
		Assists: Phil Kessel, Evgeni Malkin

THIRD PERIOD

PIT	4:16	Matt Cullen (1)
		Assists: Tom Kuhnhackl, Ian Cole
PIT	19:47	Kris Letang (1)
		Unassisted

Penguins center Evgeni Malkin (71) celebrates one of his two goals on the night. AP Photo

MIGHTY MALKIN LEADS PENGUINS PAST RANGERS

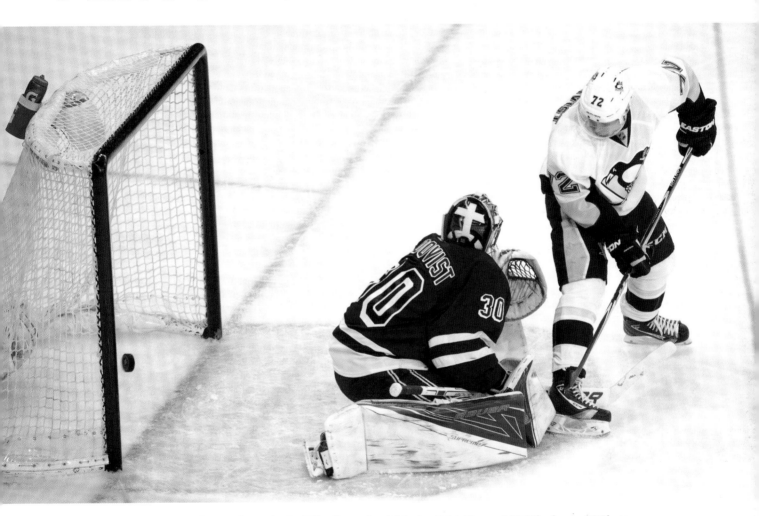

The puck slips past Rangers goalie Henrik Lundqvist (30) as Penguins right wing Patric Hornqvist (72) looks on. **AP Photo**

The Pittsburgh Penguins might have been the NHL's hottest team at the end of the regular season, playing the last month with Evgeni Malkin out of the lineup with an arm injury.

Well he's back for the playoffs, and flashing his old brilliance.

Malkin scored two goals and set up two others and the Penguins pushed the New York Rangers to the brink of playoff elimination with a 5-0 victory.

"I think he took another big step tonight," Penguins coach Mike Sullivan said. "I thought his timing was better. He's getting stronger. His conditioning is getting better with each game he's played. That is, quite honestly, what we expected to go through with Geno."

Malkin, who tied his postseason high with the

New York Rangers left winger Chris Kreider (20) misses a wide open net as Penguins goalie Matt Murray (30) attempts to make the save.
AP Photo

four points, assisted on two of the Penguins' three first-period goals in helping Pittsburgh dominate the Rangers for the second consecutive game and take a 3-1 lead in the best-of-seven, first-round series.

Sidney Crosby, who added two assists, and the red-hot Penguins can wrap up things in Game 5 in Pittsburgh.

Rookie goaltender Matt Murray, who returned to the lineup for Game 3, made 31 saves in posting his first playoff shutout.

Malkin wondered what his role would be on a team that was playing well without him.

"Of course, I thought about it when I'm not playing and the team is winning," Malkin said. "I know I can help the team. I can help the power play. This feels so much better. I know I can help this team win."

Eric Fehr, Patric Hornqvist and Conor Sheary also scored as the Penguins tallied four times on 18 shots against Henrik Lundqvist, who was lifted early in the second period.

Pittsburgh converted 3 of 6 power plays, and is 7 of 19 in the series with the extra man.

The Rangers have lost five straight home playoffs games dating to last season, and these last

March and didn't return to the lineup until Saturday, helped push the lead to 2-0 at 7:11 with a shot from the point on a power play. Crosby deflected the shot on the way in and Hornqvist tipped it again standing in front of Lundqvist for his fourth goal of the postseason.

Sheary hushed the crowd and made them start to realize this might be the final home game of the season, when he blocked a point shot by defenseman Kevin Klein, skated down the left wing and beat Lundqvist badly on a shot from the circle for a 3-0 lead at 16:12. It was his first NHL playoff goal.

By the final minute of the period time, the Penguins' near perfect play had the Rangers' fans booing the team that went to the Cup Finals two years ago and the Eastern Conference finals last season.

Malkin, who had a goal waved off late in the first period for an obvious goaltender interference call, stretched the lead to 4-0 with another power-play goal at 4:00 of the second period. It was scored with a rocket from the point after the Penguins refused to let the Rangers clear the puck out of the offensive zone.

"Geno wants to win," Sullivan said. "He's a competitive guy. He cares about this team. And he knows he's a big part of this team having success. He's a self-driven guy. He wants to be on the ice. He wants the puck in the crucial situations."

two were horrible efforts.

New York came into Game 4 vowing to pick things up after being totally outplayed in a 3-1 loss in Game 3.

They brought tenor John Amirante out of retirement to sing the national anthem and the crowd at Madison Square Garden was buzzing when the puck was dropped.

The excitement disappeared 69 seconds into the game when Lundqvist gave up a juicy rebound on a slap shot by Ben Lovejoy and Fehr charged down the middle of the ice to poke the rebound into the net. Malkin made the pass that set up Lovejoy's big shot.

The big Russian, who hurt an arm in early

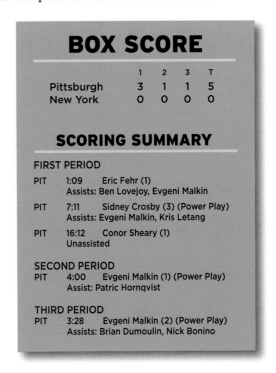

BOX SCORE

	1	2	3	T
Pittsburgh	3	1	1	5
New York	0	0	0	0

SCORING SUMMARY

FIRST PERIOD

PIT	1:09	Eric Fehr (1)
		Assists: Ben Lovejoy, Evgeni Malkin
PIT	7:11	Sidney Crosby (3) (Power Play)
		Assists: Evgeni Malkin, Kris Letang
PIT	16:12	Conor Sheary (1)
		Unassisted

SECOND PERIOD

| PIT | 4:00 | Evgeni Malkin (1) (Power Play) |
| | | Assist: Patric Hornqvist |

THIRD PERIOD

| PIT | 3:28 | Evgeni Malkin (2) (Power Play) |
| | | Assists: Brian Dumoulin, Nick Bonino |

Penguins right wing Bryan Rust (17) came up big with two goals in Game 5. AP Photo

PENGUINS KNOCK OUT RANGERS

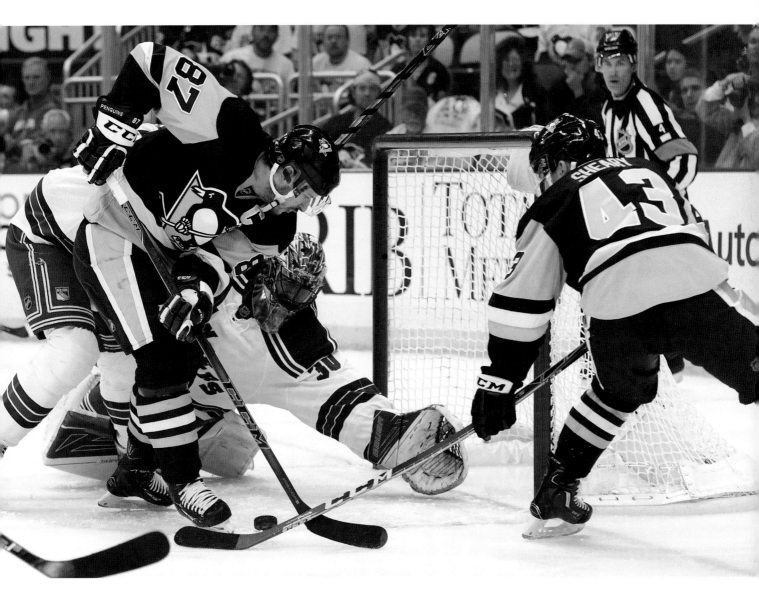

New York Rangers goalie Henrik Lundqvist (30) makes a save as Penguins center Sidney Crosby (87) and left wing Conor Sheary (43) try to play the puck in front of the net. AP Photo

The end of two springs' worth of playoff angst for the Pittsburgh Penguins came suddenly, crammed into 14 minutes of pure exhilaration, one highlight-reel sequence piled atop another.

And perhaps it's fitting that Pittsburgh's

Penguins left wing Conor Sheary (43) fires a shot for a goal during the second period. AP Photo

relentless five-game demolition of the New York Rangers, completed during a raucous 6-3 victory that ushered New York to an early offseason, wasn't sealed by the familiar faces atop the Penguins' star-laden roster, but by the pieces brought in to help return Sidney Crosby, Evgeni Malkin and Kris Letang to their spot among the league's elite.

Conor Sheary. Bryan Rust. Matt Murray. All in their early 20s. All now vital parts of a team that looks every bit a Stanley Cup contender.

Rust and Sheary combined for three goals during Pittsburgh's second-period explosion against uncharacteristically shaky Henrik Lundqvist and Murray turned away 38 shots as the Penguins exacted a bit of revenge against the Rangers, who knocked Pittsburgh out of the postseason in 2014 and 2015.

The setbacks led to franchise-wide soul searching, including hiring Mike Sullivan to take over for Mike Johnston in mid-December and having general manager Jim Rutherford overhaul the roster with fresh legs unburdened by past failure.

"We are obviously all aware of what's happened in the past," Rust said. "We wanted to fight harder to make sure that didn't happen like two years ago when the team was up 3-1 and they lost that lead and ended up losing the series."

Not by a long shot.

Matt Cullen, Carl Hagelin and Phil Kessel, who like Sheary and Rust were not on the roster when Pittsburgh bowed out in five meek games against New York last year, also scored for the Penguins to end a miserable and brief postseason for Lundqvist, who stopped just 17 of 23 shots and failed to make it to the third period for the third time in the series.

Lundqvist spent the last three games getting outplayed by Murray, 21, who turned away 85 of the 89 shots he has faced while filling in for injured starter Marc-Andre Fleury. Fleury remains out indefinitely while dealing with a concussion suffered March 31. The Penguins have won each of Murray's last 10 starts.

"I think every time you face adversity and you get through it, it definitely makes you stronger, a stronger person, stronger mentally," Murray said. "Experience is huge for us, especially us young guys."

Tied at two after the first, the Penguins simply skated by the older, slower and decidedly lethargic Rangers.

Rust gave Pittsburgh the lead for good by tapping in a pretty feed from Trevor Daley at the top of the slot, the defenseman faking a shot before sliding a pass to Rust at the doorstep 5:21 into the second. The 39-year-old Cullen doubled the Penguins' advantage just over four minutes later when Rust's aggressive forechecking took two Rangers off the puck and left it sitting there for Cullen to whip over Lundqvist's glove.

Sheary pushed it to 5-2 when Crosby skated into the New York zone, drew the Rangers' attention then fed it to the streaking Sheary, who called for the pass then zipped the puck into the top corner. By the time Rust finished off a 2-on-1 by burying a saucer pass from Malkin to give the Penguins more cushion than Murray would possibly need, the 421st consecutive sellout at Consol Energy Center was giddily chanting "Hen-rik! Hen-rik!" at the person most responsible for Pittsburgh's recent anguish.

"I think this series was a good step, we were definitely tested," Crosby said. "This should build some confidence that we can play in those games and create even when it's that tight."

BOX SCORE

	1	2	3	T
Pittsburgh	2	4	0	6
New York	2	0	1	3

SCORING SUMMARY

FIRST PERIOD
NY   1:02   Rick Nash (2)
           Assists: Dan Girardi, Brady Skjei

PIT   9:50   Carl Hagelin (1)
           Assists: Phil Kessel, Nick Bonino

NY   10:35   Dominic Moore (1)
           Assists: Jesper Fast, Marc Staal

PIT   11:39   Phil Kessel (3) (Power Play)
           Assists: Sidney Crosby, Kris Letang

SECOND PERIOD
PIT   5:21   Bryan Rust (1)
           Assists: Trevor Daley, Matt Cullen

PIT   9:26   Matt Cullen (2)
           Assists: Bryan Rust, Tom Kuhnhackl

PIT   16:18   Conor Sheary (2)
           Assist: Sidney Crosby

PIT   19:01   Bryan Rust (2)
           Assist: Evgeni Malkin

THIRD PERIOD
NY   5:38   Chris Kreider (2) (Power Play)
           Assists: Raphael Diaz, Derick Brassard

KRIS LETANG

Less than 24 hours after getting 35:22 of ice time in the Penguins' Game 2 win over the Washington Capitals in the Eastern Conference semifinals, Kris Letang was one of a handful of players participating in an optional practice.

Letang was following a carefully cultivated routine that's allowed him to spend so much time on the ice. Part of his recovery process is active exercise, and that's not something coach Mike Sullivan is going to change.

It's worked out just fine so far.

"There's not many guys out there so I can work on different things I want to do," Letang said of the extra practice time. "I have more time, more reps that I can go through. Some guys are different. They need a little more time off the ice. Some guys, they get re-energized by skating out there."

Count Letang amount the latter group. He's averaged just less than 30 minutes on the ice throughout the playoffs. In the final month of the regular season, he played more than 30 minutes five times.

So, when Olli Maatta was knocked out of Game 2 and the Penguins were left with five defensemen, it fell mostly to Letang to take on the extra minutes. He finished with a plus-2 rating.

"It's incredible," Nick Bonino said of Letang's

Kris Letang has been an iron man for the Penguins this post season. AP Photo

Letang (58) knocks down Tampa Bay Lightning center Alex Killorn (17) as he plays the puck during Game 5 of the Eastern Conference Finals. AP Photo

endurance. "I've played with some good 'D', but you see him playing 35 minutes and they aren't easy minutes. He's getting hit. He's up the ice and then back down the ice first. Especially with ony five 'D', he really carried the load back there."

"It's pretty tough. Some games you play 12 minutes and you feel like you played 25. Some guys were joking that he played three games worth of hockey for some of us last night."

Game 3 against the Capitals marked the most time Letang's spent on the ice all season, topping the 35:14 he played against Buffalo on March 29. The first and second periods were easier, he said, mostly due to power plays and the Penguins controlling the puck.

"In the third (period), you're kind of battling in front of the net, you're battling in the corner,"

he said. "It kind of drains you of your energy. You don't keep track of the minutes, but you definitely know what kinds of minutes are hard and what kinds of minutes are pretty easy."

For Letang, the road toward taking on such a substantial workload starts in the summer, where he increases his conditioning step-by-step so he's at his peak come playoff time.

"There aren't too many players I think that can handle those kinds of minutes night in and night out like Kris can," Sullivan said. "He's a very efficient player. He's a great skater. I think he's an elite defenseman.

"I've said this all along, I don't think Kris gets the type of credit he deserves for the type of defenseman that he is and the importance that he is to our team in helping this team win."

Penguins center Evgeni Malkin (71) checks Washington Capitals right wing Tom Wilson (43) into the boards. AP Photo

EASTERN CONFERENCE

CAPS TAKE 1-0 SERIES LEAD ON OSHIE'S OT GOAL

Penguins defenseman Ben Lovejoy (12) shoots and scores the Penguins first goal. AP Photo

T.J. Oshie raised his arms in celebration and looked at referee Dan O'Rourke. Oshie was pretty sure he scored in overtime to complete a hat trick and one of the biggest games of his career.

Oshie's third goal of the night stood up after video review and the Washington Capitals beat the Pittsburgh Penguins 4-3 in an overtime thriller that was a classic start to the highly anticipated second-round playoff series between Alex Ovechkin and Sidney Crosby.

Washington Capitals right wing T.J. Oshie (77) wraps the puck around the net to score the winning goal as teammate Alex Ovechkin (8) looks on. AP Photo

"That's kind of the stuff you dream about when you're a kid playing in the backyard by yourself is scoring the OT winner and getting a hat trick," Oshie said. "It was awesome. Great way to win."

Oshie's wraparound just barely crossed the goal line against the right pad of Pittsburgh's Matt Murray 9:33 into overtime. The call on the ice was a goal, and the NHL's situation room said video replay confirmed that the puck was completely over the line.

Murray, who made 31 saves but was beaten three times by Oshie and once by Andre Burakovsky, wasn't convinced.

"The ref called it a goal on the ice," Murray said. "I don't know how he could have possibly seen it from his angle. But I thought I had it, to be honest. I knew it was close, but I thought it never fully crossed the line. I thought it was close enough that it would be inconclusive."

To the Penguins, it was an inconclusive end to a fast game played at their blistering pace. Ben Lovejoy, Evgeni Malkin and Nick Bonino scored for Pittsburgh, which will try to even the best-of-seven series in Game 2.

Both teams expect much of the same entertainment value that was on display in Game 1. Beyond Murray stoning Ovechkin and Braden Holtby turning aside 42 of 45 shots, there were goals off the rush, a knee-on-knee hit by Washington's Tom Wilson on Conor Sheary and even Jay Beagle getting a stick stuck between his helmet and visor.

"The momentum shifts, the big hits, the goals, overtime, the big saves: This is what the playoffs are all about," Oshie said.

The spotlight was on Ovechkin and Crosby in their first meeting in the Stanley Cup playoffs since 2009. Ovechkin assisted on Oshie's second goal and was denied by Murray on two breakaways, while Crosby was on the ice for three goals against and won 68 percent of his faceoffs.

The Capitals won a playoff game that Holtby allowed more than two goals for the first time since Game 5 against the Boston Bruins in 2012. The Vezina Trophy finalist was tested plenty but made a big stop on Phil Kessel in the final minutes of regulation.

Pittsburgh outshot Washington 45-35.

"I thought we did a pretty good job, generated some pretty good chances," Crosby said. "I thought we had some good looks and it was a fast-paced game back and forth, a typical of a game this time of year."

Wide-open hockey led to Burakovsky's rush goal on a rebound 10:13 into the first period and to Lovejoy's similar one 10:40 into the second. That started a run of three goals in 90 seconds, which ended with Oshie's breakaway goal off a turnover by Olli Maatta.

After Oshie's third-period goal, Bonino scored with 10:18 left to help send the game to overtime. That's where Oshie was the hero, much like he was for the United States in the shootout against Russia at the 2014 Sochi Olympics.

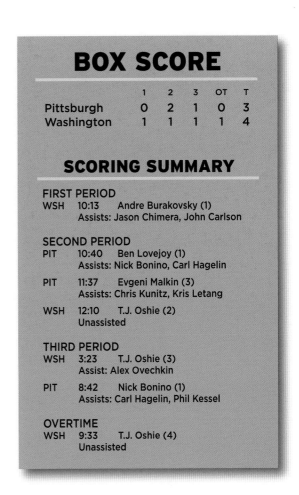

BOX SCORE

	1	2	3	OT	T
Pittsburgh	0	2	1	0	3
Washington	1	1	1	1	4

SCORING SUMMARY

FIRST PERIOD
WSH 10:13 Andre Burakovsky (1)
Assists: Jason Chimera, John Carlson

SECOND PERIOD
PIT 10:40 Ben Lovejoy (1)
Assists: Nick Bonino, Carl Hagelin

PIT 11:37 Evgeni Malkin (3)
Assists: Chris Kunitz, Kris Letang

WSH 12:10 T.J. Oshie (2)
Unassisted

THIRD PERIOD
WSH 3:23 T.J. Oshie (3)
Assist: Alex Ovechkin

PIT 8:42 Nick Bonino (1)
Assists: Carl Hagelin, Phil Kessel

OVERTIME
WSH 9:33 T.J. Oshie (4)
Unassisted

Washington Capitals defenseman Brooks Orpik (44) levels Penguins defenseman Olli Maatta (3) with a high hit during the first period. AP Photo

FEHR'S 3ᴿᴰ PERIOD GOAL HELPS PENGUINS EVEN SERIES

Penguins goalie Matt Murray (30) covers an attempt by Washington Capitals center Evgeny Kuznetsov (92). AP Photo

Already down a game in their second-round playoff series, Kris Letang and the Pittsburgh Penguins suddenly were down a man, too, when Olli Maatta was leveled by a high hit from Washington's Brooks Orpik less than 5 minutes in.

Penguins right wing Eric Fehr (16) watches his shot go past Washington Capitals goalie Braden Holtby (70) for the game winner as Brooks Orpik (44) defends. AP Photo

Inset: **Fehr (16) celebrates his goal with teammate Chris Kunitz (14). AP Photo**

So the Penguins simply did what they've been doing for weeks and weeks now: They figured out a way to set aside a setback.

Letang played more than 35 minutes to help make up for fellow defenseman Maatta's absence, and Eric Fehr scored the tiebreaking goal against his former team with about 4 1/2 minutes remaining, giving the Penguins a 2-1 victory over the Capitals that evened the

Eastern Conference series at a game apiece.

The Penguins have not lost two consecutive games since mid-January, displaying the sort of resilience that teams hope to rely on at this time of year.

"If you have that ability, you give yourself a chance every night to win. ... You've got to bounce back, and we've done a good job of that all year," Penguins star Sidney Crosby said. "Hopefully, we continue to."

Even Capitals coach Barry Trotz noted: "I sensed that they had a heightened sense of desperation."

The series shifts to Pittsburgh for Game 3. If Game 2 was any indication, it could be rough-and-tumble the rest of the way.

The tone was established early, when Orpik sent Maatta slamming to the ice. The Penguins defenseman was helped off and did not return.

"He's obviously out. We'll have more details probably tomorrow on his status," Pittsburgh coach Mike Sullivan said. "I thought it was a late hit. I thought it was a target to his head. I think it's the type of hit that everyone in hockey is trying to remove from the game. That's how I saw it."

Orpik, who helped the Penguins win a Stanley Cup when he played for them, did not speak to reporters afterward.

Trotz's take: "I'll let the league handle it. ... He's not a dirty player. The Pittsburgh people know that."

Without Maatta, Letang took on an increased role, spending more than 8 1/2 more minutes in the game than any other player on either team and helping silence Capitals captain Alex Ovechkin. In all, Pittsburgh dominated play for the first two periods, and 21-year-old rookie goalie Matt Murray finished with 23 saves.

"To play with five `D' for as long as we had to ... that wasn't easy," Crosby said. "They were the difference in us winning tonight."

Fehr helped, of course. He redirected a pass out of a corner from Evgeni Malkin, sending the puck off the right post and past goalie Braden Holtby. Fehr played parts of nine seasons in Washington across two stints before leaving as a free agent last summer.

"It does feel a little bit different" than other big goals, Fehr said, adding: "Obviously, I had a lot of years here."

Carl Hagelin put Pittsburgh ahead in the second period, before Marcus Johansson pulled Washington even on a power play with about 16 minutes to go in the third.

Pittsburgh recovered quickly from its 4-3 overtime loss in Game 1, dominating play for stretches and taking 12 of the game's first 13 shots.

"That was too easy of a game through the first 40 (minutes), probably, for them," Capitals defenseman Matt Niskanen said through a bloody lip.

Said Ovechkin: "Didn't play how we want to play."

BOX SCORE

	1	2	3	T
Pittsburgh	0	1	1	2
Washington	0	0	1	1

SCORING SUMMARY

SECOND PERIOD
PIT   7:08   Carl Hagelin (2)
         Assist: Nick Bonino

THIRD PERIOD
WSH   4:08   Marcus Johansson (2) (Power Play)
         Assists: John Carlson, Evgeny Kuznetsov

PIT   15:32   Eric Fehr (2)
         Assists: Evgeni Malkin, Chris Kunitz

Washington Capitals right wing Tom Wilson (43) and Penguins defenseman Kris Letang (58) have words after the action has stopped during the first period. AP Photo

EASTERN CONFERENCE

SEMI-FINALS MAY 2, 2016 CONSOL ENERGY CENTER PITTSBURGH, PENNSYLVANIA

PITTSBURGH PENGUINS 3 • WASHINGTON CAPITALS 2

MURRAY, PENS TOP CAPS FOR 2-1 SERIES LEAD

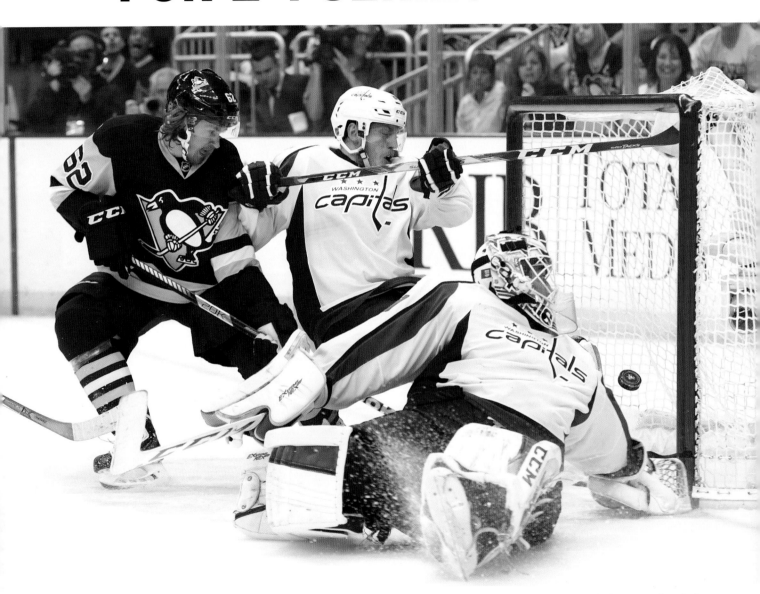

Penguins left wing Carl Hagelin (62) scores the game winner past Washington Capitals goalie Braden Holtby (70) during second period action. AP Photo

Rookie goaltender Matt Murray made 47 stops, and the Pittsburgh Penguins did just enough counter punching to edge the Washington Capitals 3-2 for a 2-1 lead in an increasingly fractious best-of-seven series that is living up to its billing.

Penguins goalie Matt Murray (30) comes up big with a glove save on a point blank shot by Washington Capitals T.J. Oshie (77). **AP Photo**

Patric Hornqvist and Tom Kuhnhackl scored a minute apart in the first period, Carl Hagelin added his third of the playoffs in the second, and the Penguins held on despite relentless pressure from the Capitals. Alex Ovechkin and Justin Williams scored in the third, but the Capitals find themselves in a deficit against a franchise they have beaten just once in eight previous playoff meetings.

"They throw a lot of pucks at the net, and without Murray, there's no way we win this game," Hornqvist said.

The Penguins might have to play without Kris Letang. The star defenseman earned a two-minute minor for interference in the first period after launching himself at Washington's

Marcus Johansson in a sequence that had some of the same hallmarks of the hit that earned Washington's Brooks Orpik a three-game suspension for drilling Olli Maatta in Game 2.

Johansson was skating into the offensive zone late in the first period when he was headed off by four Penguins. The puck was steered away and long gone by the time Letang turned toward Johansson and nailed him.

Unlike Maatta, Johansson was able to return, although he doesn't believe that should absolve Letang.

"He obviously leaves his feet and hits me in the head," Johansson said. "That's the kinds of plays you want out of the league. It doesn't look good."

Neither does the way the series looks at the moment for Washington, which had a 49-23 advantage in shots and collected 33 more hits than the Penguins (58-25).

The NHL's best team during the regular season has just three goals in the past six periods against Murray, who is playing so well Marc-Andre Fleury might want to get used to his spot on the bench.

Wearing the same Pittsburgh gold uniforms that team owner Mario Lemieux wore during the club's consecutive Stanley Cup runs in 1991 and 1992 -- runs that included victories over Washington -- it seemed like old times for the Penguins, who counter attacked brilliantly.

Sidney Crosby keyed a rush that ended with Conor Sheary chasing down a blocked shot in the corner and feeding it to Trevor Daley at the point. Hornqvist reached out and expertly smacked the puck off the ice, allowing it to skid right by Braden Holtby to give Pittsburgh a lead perhaps it didn't deserve just 6:37 into the game.

A minute later, Washington's deficit doubled when Nicklas Backstrom whiffed while trying to intercept Letang's long stretch pass to Matt Cullen. The ensuing 2-on-1 ended with the puck smacking off Kuhnhackl's back and into the net.

Nate Schmidt opened the door for the Penguins to make it 3-0 late in the second period, flipping a blind backhand pass deep in the Washington end into the slot. Two passes later, Hagelin was tipping in a slick feed from Nick Bonino, who drew Holtby out, and then tucked the puck around the sprawled goaltender to Hagelin in front of the open net.

Ovechkin's fourth of the postseason, a blur that whizzed by Murray's mask 8:02 into the third, gave Washington momentum, but there wasn't enough time to catch up. Williams scored with 56 seconds remaining and the Capitals managed a couple more chances in the waning moments but couldn't sneak anything by Murray.

"I thought Murray was the reason they had success," Washington coach Barry Trotz said.

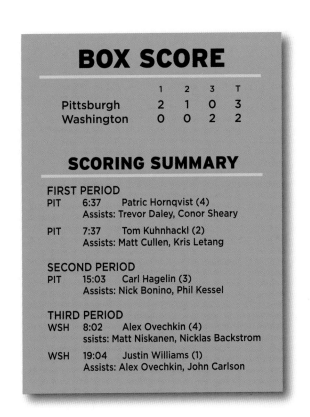

BOX SCORE

	1	2	3	T
Pittsburgh	2	1	0	3
Washington	0	0	2	2

SCORING SUMMARY

FIRST PERIOD
PIT   6:37   Patric Hornqvist (4)
            Assists: Trevor Daley, Conor Sheary

PIT   7:37   Tom Kuhnhackl (2)
            Assists: Matt Cullen, Kris Letang

SECOND PERIOD
PIT   15:03   Carl Hagelin (3)
            Assists: Nick Bonino, Phil Kessel

THIRD PERIOD
WSH   8:02   Alex Ovechkin (4)
            ssists: Matt Niskanen, Nicklas Backstrom

WSH   19:04   Justin Williams (1)
            Assists: Alex Ovechkin, John Carlson

PENGUIN ROOKIES

It's easy to get awestruck the first time a new face walks into the Pittsburgh Penguins dressing room.

All those stars. All those glittering resumes. All that talent. Hey, there's Sidney Crosby. Hey, there's Evgeni Malkin. Hey, there's Kris Letang. Coach Mike Sullivan understands it can be a little overwhelming at first.

"When a new player comes to our team, young or old for that matter, I think there's a little bit of a 'wow' factor because some of the players we have," Sullivan said. "Everybody has so much respect for Crosby and Malkin and Letang and those guys. Over time I think that wears off."

If the Penguins wanted to get where they are now — two wins away from the franchise's fourth Stanley Cup — it had to. Fast.

Fortunately, Conor Sheary, Matt Murray, Bryan Rust and Tom Kuhnhackl are quick studies. The rookies — all of whom spent a significant portion of the season with the team's American Hockey League affiliate on the other side of the state in Wilkes-Barre/Scranton — have found their footing alongside their high-profile teammates during Pittsburgh's race through the playoffs and into the Stanley Cup Final.

There's the seemingly unshakeable if impossibly thin 22-year-old Murray, who has for now (and perhaps for good) supplanted Marc-Andre Fleury in net. Murray's 13 postseason victories are a team record for a rookie and two shy of the NHL mark of 15 shared by Hall of Famer Patrick Roy, among others.

There's the undersized (5-foot-8) and yet redoubtable 23-year-old Sheary, thrust onto a line with Crosby because of his ability to skate as if he's worried the ice will melt underneath him if he stops. All he's done is pump in four goals during the playoffs, including the overtime winner in Game 2 of the Stanley Cup.

There's the 24-year-old Rust, who has a flair for the dramatic. His six goals over 19 playoff games — compared to five in 55 regular season games — include a pair in a series closeout win over the New York Rangers in April and the game-winning marker in Game 7 of the Eastern Conference finals against Tampa Bay.

There's the responsible Kuhnhackl, an intelligent penalty killer who opts for the smart play instead of the spectacular one.

All four in the midst of their first seasons in the league. All four uncowed by the moment.

"I think they've been thrown into a lot of different scenarios," Crosby said. "They're handling it really well and they're coming up big for us."

Thanks in no small part to the leadership of players like Crosby, who have made it a point to make the youngsters feel included, be it for a team meal on the road or a little post practice confab to share tricks of the trade.

The Wilkes-Barre crew is in Pittsburgh with no plans on making the trip back east anytime soon. If ever.

"A lot of us have been together for a long time here, starting in Wilkes and making our way up here," Murray said. "We're all pretty close friends and it's fun to be on this ride with all of them."

Left:Penguins right wing Bryan Rust (17) looks to turn the corner on his way to the goal. AP Photo

Right: Penguins right wing Tom Kuhnhackl (34) skates the puck around Washington Capitals defenseman Karl Alzner (27). AP Photo

Left: Penguins Conor Sheary (43) controls the puck against the San Jose Sharks. AP Photo

Right: Penguins goalie Matt Murray (30) prepares to make a save. AP Photo

Washington Capitals defenseman Taylor Chorney (4) checks Penguins center Sidney Crosby (87) off the puck during the third period. AP Photo

HORNQVIST OT WINNER GIVES PENS 3-1 SERIES LEAD

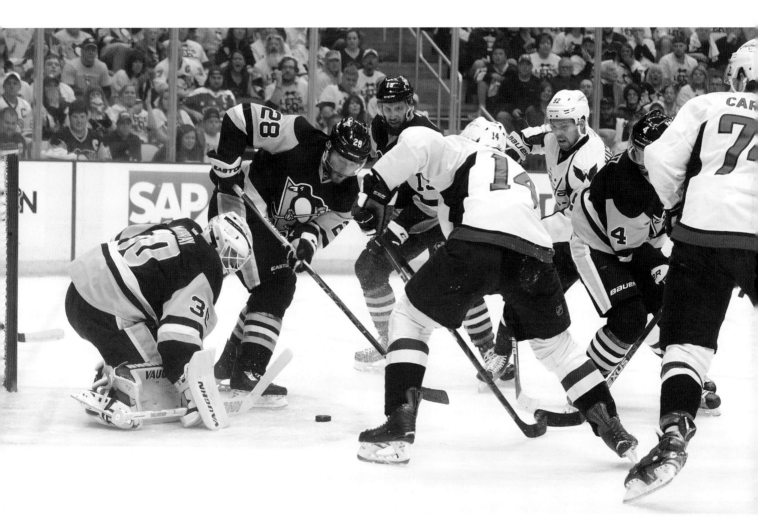

Penguins goalie Matt Murray (30) makes a tough save on Washington Capitals right wing Justin Williams (14). AP Photo

Penguins forward Patric Hornqvist fired a loose puck between Braden Holtby's legs 2:34 into overtime to give the Penguins a 3-2 victory over the Washington Capitals in Game 4 of the tightly contested second-round series.

Washington's Mike Weber tried to steer the puck out of harm's way in front of the net, but it went right to Hornqvist charging in from the right circle. Hornqvist buried it for his fifth goal of the postseason to give the Penguins a 3-1 lead in the best-of-seven Eastern Conference semifinals.

"That's a big win," Hornqvist said. "Now we have to stick with it. We haven't done anything yet."

Maybe, but the Penguins can advance to

Penguins right wing Patric Hornqvist (72) scores the game winning goal in overtime.   AP Photo

the conference final with a victory in Game 5 in Washington on Saturday after sending the Capitals to a third straight loss.

"We have to have the mentality shift by shift, period by period, try to turn it around," said Washington captain Alex Ovechkin, who had seven of his team's 36 shots but was held without a point.

The Penguins survived despite missing defenseman Kris Letang, serving a one-game suspension for an illegal hit on Marcus Johansson

in Game 3. The makeshift group at the blue line that included Brian Dumoulin and Justin Schultz played just fine in the absence of perhaps Pittsburgh's most indispensable player. The Penguins blocked 14 shots and clogged the area in front of the net to protect rookie goaltender Matt Murray.

"It wasn't a perfect game by any stretch, but we're playing against a pretty good opponent, and Tanger's a tough guy to replace," Pittsburgh coach Mike Sullivan said. "Guys had to play more minutes,

borderline moments, but Crosby said he feels that's part of playoff hockey.

"It's intense. It's physical," he said. "I think it's normal when each game goes along. You watch the other games, and it's very similar. I don't think it's anything out of the ordinary, but [it has] picked up each game."

Pittsburgh had been on the wrong end of sudden-death overtime eight straight times since beating the New York Islanders in Game 6 of the first round in 2013. The drought ended when a Conor Sheary shot from the point was stopped by Weber before it got to Holtby. Weber then nudged it across the slot to an awaiting Hornqvist. Holtby, who was focusing on Crosby standing right in front of him, couldn't get his legs closed fast enough.

"I have to get over there quicker than I did," Holtby said.

The Capitals now have to rally from a 3-1 deficit, something they've done only twice in the franchise's 41 seasons.

"A lot of us have been on both sides of the 3-1 series," Crosby said. "I think you understand that when you have a team in that position you have to take advantage of it."

BOX SCORE

	1	2	3	OT	T
Pittsburgh	1	1	0	1	3
Washington	1	1	0	0	2

SCORING SUMMARY

FIRST PERIOD
WSH 2:58 Jay Beagle (3)
Assists: Tom Wilson, Taylor Chorney

PIT 9:16 Trevor Daley (1)
Assists: Patric Hornqvist, Sidney Crosby

SECOND PERIOD
PIT 3:07 Matt Cullen (3)
Assists: Tom Kuhnhackl, Brian Dumoulin

WSH 16:19 T.J. Oshie (6) (Power Play)
Assists: Nicklas Backstrom, Alex Ovechkin

OVERTIME
PIT 2:34 Patric Hornqvist (5)
Assists: Conor Sheary, Brian Dumoulin

more significant roles. I thought the group of them did a tremendous job."

Matt Cullen and Trevor Daley also scored for Pittsburgh, and Murray stopped 34 shots to improve to 13-1 in his last 14 starts, including a 6-1 mark in the postseason. Penguins captain Sidney Crosby left briefly in the third period after getting slashed by Ovechkin, but his presence early in overtime helped set up the winner.

The series has had its share of nasty and

Washington Capitals right wing Justin Williams (14) collides with Penguins defenseman Kris Letang (58). AP Photo

EASTERN CONFERENCE

SEMI-FINALS MAY 7, 2016 VERIZON CENTER DISTRICT OF COLUMBIA, WASHINGTON

PITTSBURGH PENGUINS 1 ● WASHINGTON CAPITALS 3

OVECHKIN KEEPS CAPS SEASON ALIVE

Chris Kunitz (14) scores the Penguins only goal of the game during the first period. AP Photo

Alex Ovechkin's teammates watched him turn his game up to a whole new level. Then the Capitals followed him all the way to Game 6.

With Alex Ovechkin leading the way, the Washington Capitals beat the Pittsburgh Penguins 3-1 in Game 5 to keep their season

Penguins center Nick Bonino (13) checks Washington Capitals left wing Andre Burakovsky (65) off his feet. AP Photo

alive. Ovechkin scored a power-play goal, assisted on T.J. Oshie's and was a force all over the ice with his team on the verge of yet another early playoff exit.

"He's our leader. We look up to him," Oshie said. "When you see a guy like him that can beat you in so many different ways come out and bring that type of energy, you'd better get on board or just stay on the bench."

Behind Ovechkin's two-point game, goals by Oshie and Justin Williams and 30 saves by Braden Holtby, Washington cut its deficit to 3-2 to force Game 6 on Tuesday night in Pittsburgh.

Ovechkin looked like a man determined not to let the Capitals go quietly into the offseason. Washington's captain was quietly confident and said the belief never wavered inside the locker room.

"We didn't want to give up," Ovechkin said. "When we have pressure, it's kind of our time.

The guys responded well."

Ovechkin keyed that response, scoring 4:04 in to snap the Capitals out of a power-play drought that threatened to cost them the series. He also had the big shot that rebounded off Penguins goalie Matt Murray and to Oshie for his power-play goal in the second period.

The power play, which was 1-for-12 in the first four games, did enough to offset Pittsburgh's first power-play goal of the series, scored by Chris Kunitz in the first period. Williams added an insurance goal to wake from his postseason slumber, and Holtby did the rest.

Turning in a brilliant performance worthy of his status as a Vezina Trophy finalist, Holtby was stellar and at his best when he stopped three in a less than minute from Evgeni Malkin, Patric Hornqvist and Justin Schultz.

"That's why he's the best goalie in the league," Ovechkin said.

That succession of saves by body, pads and glove late in the second period drew a standing ovation and chants of "Holtby! Holtby!" from the sellout crowd at Verizon Center hoping it wasn't seeing its final game of the season.

Holtby wasn't happy with his play in Game 4 on Wednesday night and more than redeemed himself as the Penguins outshot the Capitals 31-19.

"I wanted to make a difference for our team, show that I would rebound just like all of us," Holtby said. "Some nights you can make those saves."

Murray wasn't at his sharpest, looking like a rookie for the first time in the Stanley Cup playoffs.

"I got outplayed, and that was the difference in the game," said Murray, who stopped 104 of 109 shots in Games 2-4.

Murray was also victimized on a brutal turnover by defenseman Brian Dumoulin that led to Williams' second-period goal.

"I'm sure he'd like to have that one back," Pittsburgh coach Mike Sullivan said of Dumoulin's costly giveaway.

Despite breaking their 0-for-14 power-play spell in the series, the Penguins couldn't close out the Capitals in five games like they did the New York Rangers in the first round. Six penalties had them lamenting a missed opportunity.

"We can't give their power play as many opportunities as we did," Crosby said. "We haven't taken a lot of penalties all playoffs long, and now isn't the time to start."

The Capitals will take all the power-play chances they can get after finishing fifth in the NHL in that department during the regular season. After the power play got clicking, there's now no shortage of belief that they can erase a 3-1 deficit for the first time since 2009.

Coach Barry Trotz told his assistant coaches before the game: "We're winning tonight, there's no question." Trotz was then eager to try to shelve this victory and put the focus on Game 6.

His players are already thinking that way after fending off elimination.

"We stopped it once. Now we need to do it twice more," Williams said.

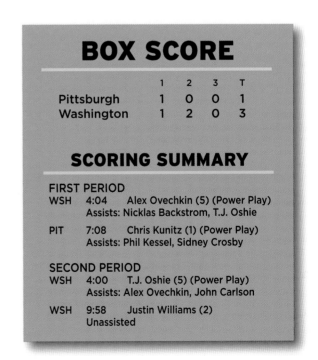

BOX SCORE

	1	2	3	T
Pittsburgh	1	0	0	1
Washington	1	2	0	3

SCORING SUMMARY

FIRST PERIOD
WSH   4:04   Alex Ovechkin (5) (Power Play)
Assists: Nicklas Backstrom, T.J. Oshie

PIT   7:08   Chris Kunitz (1) (Power Play)
Assists: Phil Kessel, Sidney Crosby

SECOND PERIOD
WSH   4:00   T.J. Oshie (5) (Power Play)
Assists: Alex Ovechkin, John Carlson

WSH   9:58   Justin Williams (2)
Unassisted

Penguins Nick Bonino (13) is mobbed by teammates after scoring the winning goal in overtime. AP Photo

EASTERN CONFERENCE

SEMI-FINALS MAY 10, 2016 CONSOL ENERGY CENTER PITTSBURGH, PENNSYLVANIA

PITTSBURGH PENGUINS 4 ● WASHINGTON CAPITALS 3

IN THE NICK OF TIME PENS SEND CAPS PACKING

Nick Bonino (13) tips in a rebound for the game winner in front of the Capitals Nicklas Backstrom (19) and Matt Niskanen (2). AP Photo

Keep skating. Play fast. Be confident. Those were the instructions from Pittsburgh Penguins coach Mike Sullivan to his team as they headed to overtime in Game 6 against the Washington Capitals.

In the span of a dozen frantic seconds early in the extra period, Carl Hagelin, Phil Kessel and Nick Bonino did all three, sending their resilient club to the Eastern Conference final in the process.

Bonino tapped in a rebound of Hagelin's shot by Braden Holtby 6:32 into overtime to give

Penguins Phil Kessel (81) shoots and scores a power play goal on Capitals goalie Braden Holtby during second period action. Teammate Sidney Crosby (87) looks on. AP Photo

the Penguins a 4-3 win to wrap up the series in six games and set up a showdown with Tampa Bay for the right to play for the Stanley Cup.

Kessel went to the corner to retrieve the puck and passed it to Hagelin in the slot. Hagelin's shot caromed off Holtby's right pad directly to Bonino, who had little trouble pushing it into the net for his 10th career playoff goal, and easily his most important.

"I just went to the front," Bonino said. "The puck always ends up there and I was able to get a stick on it. It wasn't pretty, but they're usually not."

Not that style points mattered much. The Capitals overcame a three-goal deficit in the final 22 minutes of regulation and earned a break when Jay Beagle went to his belly on the goal line to steer a shot by Patric Hornqvist out of harm's way early in the extra period.

There was no stopping Bonino's tap-in, however, sending the Presidents' Trophy winners to their dressing room with an all-too familiar feeling.

Nine times the longtime rivals have met in the

Pittsburgh, including the shot that allowed Bonino to send Consol Energy Center into a frenzy.

"I thought we did a really good job on Crosby and Malkin the whole series, but a lot of the other people hurt us," Washington coach Barry Trotz said.

T.J. Oshie, Justin Williams and John Carlson scored during Washington's comeback, one completed after three straight delay of game penalties against the Penguins gave one of the league's best power plays enough time to tie it up.

Chris Kunitz, Ian Cole and Bonino all flipped the puck over the glass from the defensive zone in a span of 2:02, a sequence that led to Carlson's fifth playoff goal, a shot that bounced and skipped by Murray to provide another compelling twist in a series that lived up to -- and perhaps beyond -- its billing.

Sullivan tried to remain upbeat in the dressing room before the third overtime game of the series.

"What we talked about was taking a deep breath, not changing what's happened and letting it go," he said. "These guys to their credit have done an amazing job of not allowing any sort of ebbs and flows of the game to affect them."

playoffs. Eight times the post-series handshake line has ended with Pittsburgh celebrating while Washington trudges toward the offseason.

Thanks in part to an inability to keep Bonino, Hagelin and Kessel in check. While Washington kept Pittsburgh stars Sidney Crosby and Evgeni Malkin under wraps -- they combined for all of four points in six games -- the Capitals struggled to keep up with one of the fastest lines in the league.

Kessel scored twice and helped set up the winner. Hagelin added a goal and two assists for

BOX SCORE

	1	2	3	OT	T
Pittsburgh	1	2	0	1	4
Washington	0	1	2	0	3

SCORING SUMMARY

FIRST PERIOD
PIT   5:41   Phil Kessel (4)
            Assists: Brian Dumoulin, Carl Hagelin

SECOND PERIOD
PIT   7:05   Phil Kessel (5) (Power Play)
            Assists: Kris Letang, Chris Kunitz

PIT   7:38   Carl Hagelin (4) (Power Play)
            Assists: Olli Maatta, Trevor Daley

WSH   18:30   T.J. Oshie (6) (Power Play)
            Assists: Nicklas Backstrom, Alex Ovechkin

THIRD PERIOD
WSH   7:23   Justin Williams (3)
            Assist: Nicklas Backstrom

WSH   13:10   John Carlson (5) (Power Play)
            Assists: Alex Ovechkin, Justin Williams

OVERTIME
PIT   6:32   Nick Bonino (2)
            Assists: Carl Hagelin, Phil Kessel

Penguins goalie Matt Murray (30) reaches to glove a loose puck as Caps players look for the rebound. AP Photo

Two NHL greats - Sidney Crosby and Alex Ovechkin – show each other mutual respect after the 4-3 overtime Penguins win clinched the series. AP Photo

PHIL KESSEL

For a kid from Madison, Wisc., who just likes to score goals, Phil Kessel has been through a lot in his NHL career.

He had to deal with testicular cancer at the beginning. And at times he either electrified or disappointed fan-bases in Boston and Toronto. He's been feted and demonized. Chants of "Thank you, Kessel!" meant two different things to fans in Boston and Toronto.

The speedy winger's been called a coach killer. He heard former coach Ron Wilson declare: "You can't win with Phil." And Kessel has just been left off Team USA's entry in hockey's World Cup despite a magnificent playoffs with the Pittsburgh Penguins that has him in the conversation for the Conn Smythe Trophy.

In 18 playoff games thus far he has nine goals and nine assists, tied for fifth in post-season scoring.

"I think throughout your life and your career, little moments shape your life and who you are," Kessel said. "And I think I am who I am because of what's happened in my life. I'm happy to be here and be part of this."

Kessel is four wins away from being a Stanley Cup champion — unthinkable during his days with the Maple Leafs.

"It's been fun," said Kessel. "Obviously, I never got a chance to play in the Stanley Cup like this. I've never been on a team that has felt like this. I don't even know how to describe it, to be honest. I'm so excited to play for the Stanley Cup."

The improvement in the overall game of Phil Kessel (81) has been instrumental in the Pens Stanley Cup run. AP Photo

Kessel (81) fires the puck on goal during Game 1 of the Stanley Cup. AP Photo

Kessel seemed remarkably relaxed at the podium Stanley Cup media day. The scrum around Kessel — filled with familiar faces of the media—was one of the day's biggest.

It's understandable, because Kessel is an enigma, a hockey-playing savant. He'd come to the Leafs at the famously high cost of three draft picks — two of them first-rounders — and the pressure was on him from the get-go.

He produced, though, and was the team's leading scorer in all six of his seasons in Toronto. And he was the best player on the ice for either team during the Leafs' only playoff appearance during his tenure, a seven-game loss to the Boston Bruins.

But he was booed out of town, deemed an uncaring, under-achiever who could be so much better if he only worked harder.

The Penguins, though, are happy to have Kessel, whose speed and scoring ability on the third line can be such a difference-maker. Teams understandably try to shut down Sidney Crosby's line first, and Evgeni Malkin's line second when handling the Penguins.

"Phil deserves the credit for how his game has evolved over the course of this season," said Penguins coach Mike Sullivan. "He has made a commitment level to this team that all of us respect and admire. I know we would not be playing in the Stanley Cup final without his contributions.

"He has scored some big goals for us at key times down the stretch and in the post-season. Phil is enjoying this team. He's enjoying his teammates and the role he has evolved into as part of this group."

Kessel, with Nick Bonino and Carl Hagelin, forms a potent third line.

"He's a funny guy, and as the season has gone on we've gotten closer," Hagelin said of Kessel. "On the ice, we have some chemistry. It's great for a player like me to play with a player like him who can shoot the puck, and also make plays."

Kessel admitted it hurt not to be included in Team USA's World Cup lineup. But he might yet get the last laugh.

"Obviously you're a little disappointed, but it is what it is," said Kessel. "I've had a pretty good playoffs and I've always done pretty well for them in all the tournaments I've played for them. But we're in the Stanley Cup final, so I can't be too disappointed."

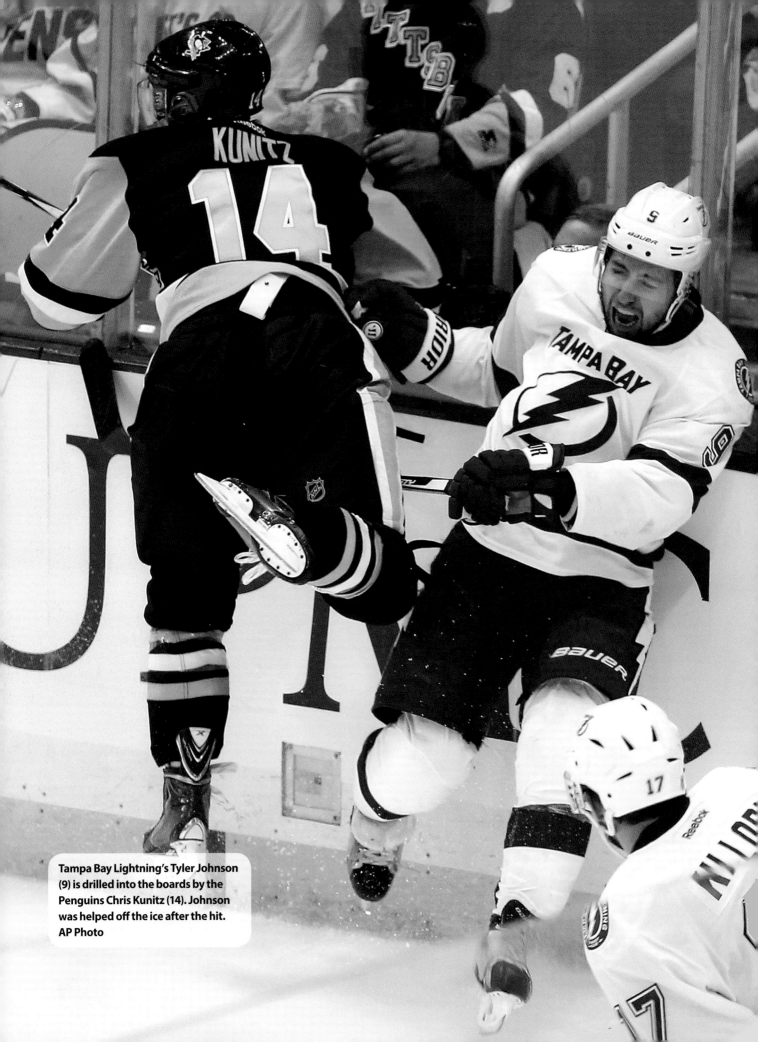

Tampa Bay Lightning's Tyler Johnson (9) is drilled into the boards by the Penguins Chris Kunitz (14). Johnson was helped off the ice after the hit.
AP Photo

LIGHTNING DOWN PENGUINS IN SERIES OPENER

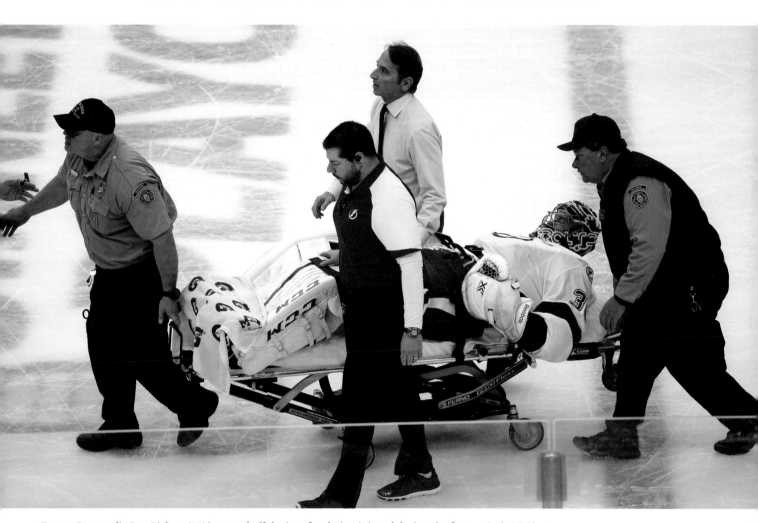

Tampa Bay goalie Ben Bishop (30) is carted off the ice after being injured during the first period. AP Photo

When Tampa Bay goaltender and Vezina Trophy finalist Ben Bishop left Game 1 of the Eastern Conference finals in the first period with a left leg injury, the Lightning wished him well and went right back to work.

Andrei Vasilevskiy made 25 stops filling in, and Tampa Bay bottled up the Pittsburgh Penguins for a 3-1 victory to seize home-ice advantage in the best-of-seven series.

"I think we played well even before (Bishop's injury), and we kept going," said forward Ondrej Palat, who scored his third goal of the postseason. "We know Vasi is a really good goalie."

One Tampa Bay might have to rely on with

Lightning goalie Andrei Vasilevskiy (88) stops a point blank shot by the Penguins Sidney Crosby (87). AP Photo

Bishop's situation uncertain.

Bishop, the massive, 6-foot-7 anchor at the back end of the Lightning defense, left on a stretcher 12:25 into the series after his left leg wrenched awkwardly underneath him as he tried to scramble back into position.

The Lightning dropped just two games while sprinting to their second straight appearance in the conference finals despite missing franchise center Steven Stamkos and top defenseman Anton Stralman, both of whom remain out indefinitely with health issues.

The meeting between two of the fastest teams in the league was supposed to play in stark contrast to Pittsburgh's physical six-game series with Washington. The anticipated track meet never materialized, and the scoring chances created off the rush were one-sided in favor of the Lightning.

net 18:25 into the second period to give the Lightning complete command.

Facing just its second three-goal deficit of the playoffs, Pittsburgh drew within two on Patric Hornqvist's power-play goal with just 55 seconds left in the second, a shot from the right circle set up by a pretty, between-the-legs flick by Sidney Crosby. While the score seemed to give the Penguins a decided lift -- they carried the play over much of the final 20 minutes -- the Lightning and Vasilevskiy held on to grab the early momentum in a series that looks far more contentious going forward than it appeared going in.

"I don't think they saw our best today," Penguins coach Mike Sullivan said.

Pittsburgh insisted it was a far different team than the one that lost all three regular-season meetings to the Lightning, pointing to the club's strong finish and heady play while dispatching the Rangers and Capitals in this season's playoffs. The Penguins proved they were much improved over the group Tampa Bay last saw Feb. 20.

Maybe, but the Lightning tested that mettle early when Ryan Callahan crunched Pittsburgh's Kris Letang in the corner less than three minutes in, sending the star defenseman slumping to the ice. Letang was motionless for a moment before eventually skating to the locker room. Callahan received a major penalty for boarding but remained in the game, and Letang made a surprisingly quick return during the lengthy delay as Bishop was stretchered off.

Tampa Bay struck 18:46 into the first, when Alex Killorn slipped behind struggling Pittsburgh defenseman Olli Maatta and fit a shot between Matt Murray's legs. Palat doubled the lead 2:33 into the second, when Valtteri Filppula's slap shot smacked off Murray's pads and -- with no Penguins around to get in his way -- Palat reached out and slammed home the rebound. Jonathan Drouin finished off a 3-on-2 by burying a feed from Palat into the open

BOX SCORE

	1	2	3	T
Pittsburgh	0	1	0	1
Tampa Bay	1	2	0	3

SCORING SUMMARY

FIRST PERIOD
TB   18:46   Alex Killorn (4)
                   Assist: Victor Hedman

SECOND PERIOD
TB   2:33   Ondrej Palat (3) (Power Play)
                   Assists: Valtteri Filppula, Jason Garrison

TB   18:25   Jonathan Drouin (2)
                   Assists: Ondrej Palat, Valtteri Filppula

PIT   19:05   Patric Hornqvist (6) (Power Play)
                   Assists: Sidney Crosby, Phil Kessel

Penguins captain Sidney Crosby, second from left, celebrates with teammates Matt Cullen (7), Brian Dumoulin (8), Kris Letang (58) and Patric Hornqvist, right, after scoring the game winning goal in overtime. AP Photo

CROSBY'S OT WINNER EVENS SERIES

Lightning goalie Andrei Vasilevskiy makes a save on a blast from Sidney Crosby (87). AP Photo

Sidney Crosby wasn't sure Bryan Rust saw him, so the Pittsburgh Penguins captain gave his impromptu linemate a quick yell just to make sure.

"I tried to let him know I was there," Crosby said.

A deft drop pass from Rust and a flick of Crosby's wrist later, the superstar's lengthy postseason scoring drought was over. So were the chances of the Penguins falling into a deep hole against Tampa Bay in the Eastern Conference finals.

Crosby's shot sailed high and hard over Andrei Vasilevskiy's stick 40 seconds into overtime, lifting the Penguins to a 3-2 victory and tying the best-of-seven series at 1.

"It feels good to get rewarded," Crosby said after collecting the first overtime playoff winner of his NHL career. "I feel we deserved it tonight."

Crosby hadn't found the back of the net since Game 4 of the opening round against the New York Rangers.

In danger of heading south down 2-0, Crosby generated scoring chance after scoring chance, including a backhand in the second period that appeared destined for an open net before Vasilevskiy stretched his glove out to make a save that could have tilted the balance of power in the series.

Instead, it only seemed to lift the Penguins to another level. Pittsburgh dominated most of the night, outshooting Tampa Bay 41-21 while spending most of the game in the Lightning zone. Only the brilliant play of the 21-year-old Vasilevskiy -- filling in for injured starter Ben Bishop -- kept Tampa Bay in it.

Vasilevskiy finished with 38 stops, but darted toward the dressing room after he moved too far to his left when squaring to face Crosby, giving Crosby all the room he needed to score perhaps the second-most important goal of his life after his overtime winner for Team Canada in the gold medal game of the 2010 Olympics.

That goal proved cathartic for his home country. This one could do the same for Crosby's adopted city, one in desperate need of a Stanley Cup to bookend the one Crosby helped claim in 2009.

The Penguins still haven't lost consecutive games of any variety since January and none with the usual allotment of men on the ice since coach Mike Sullivan's first week on the job back in December.

"We just stayed with it," Sullivan said. "We tried to play the game the right way. That's what I like the most about the group. As the game wore on we got better and better."

Matt Cullen and Phil Kessel scored during Pittsburgh's two-goal burst to start the game and Matt Murray rebounded from a shaky start to finish with 19 saves, including stuffing Alex Killorn on a breakaway

late in the second period of a tie game.

"It was a huge save, there's no doubt," Sullivan said. "Matt's history has been he's always responded pretty solid when he thinks he could have had one or would have liked one back."

Anton Stralman scored in his return to the lineup from a fractured left leg and Jonathan Drouin picked up his second goal of the series,

Penguins goalie Matt Murray (30) makes a save as Lightning center Jonathan Marchessault (81) sets up in front to tip the puck. AP Photo

but the Lightning lost for just the third time in 12 postseason games.

The Penguins pointed to an inability to generate quality chances from in close as a major problem in Game 1. In danger of falling behind by two games for the first time in the postseason, Pittsburgh wasted little time trying to make Vasilevskiy uncomfortable, scoring a pair of early goals on scrambles from in front to go up 2-0 less than 10 minutes in.

BOX SCORE

	1	2	3	OT	T
Pittsburgh	2	0	0	1	3
Tampa Bay	2	0	0	0	2

SCORING SUMMARY

FIRST PERIOD

PIT   4:32   Matt Cullen (4)
Assists: Eric Fehr, Kris Letang

PIT   9:37   Phil Kessel (6)
Assists: Nick Bonino, Carl Hagelin

TB   16:37   Anton Stralman (1)
Assists: Jonathan Marchessault, Victor Hedman

TB   19:10   Jonathan Drouin (3)
Assists: J.T. Brown, Matt Carle

OVERTIME

PIT   0:40   Sidney Crosby (4)
Assists: Bryan Rust, Brian Dumoulin

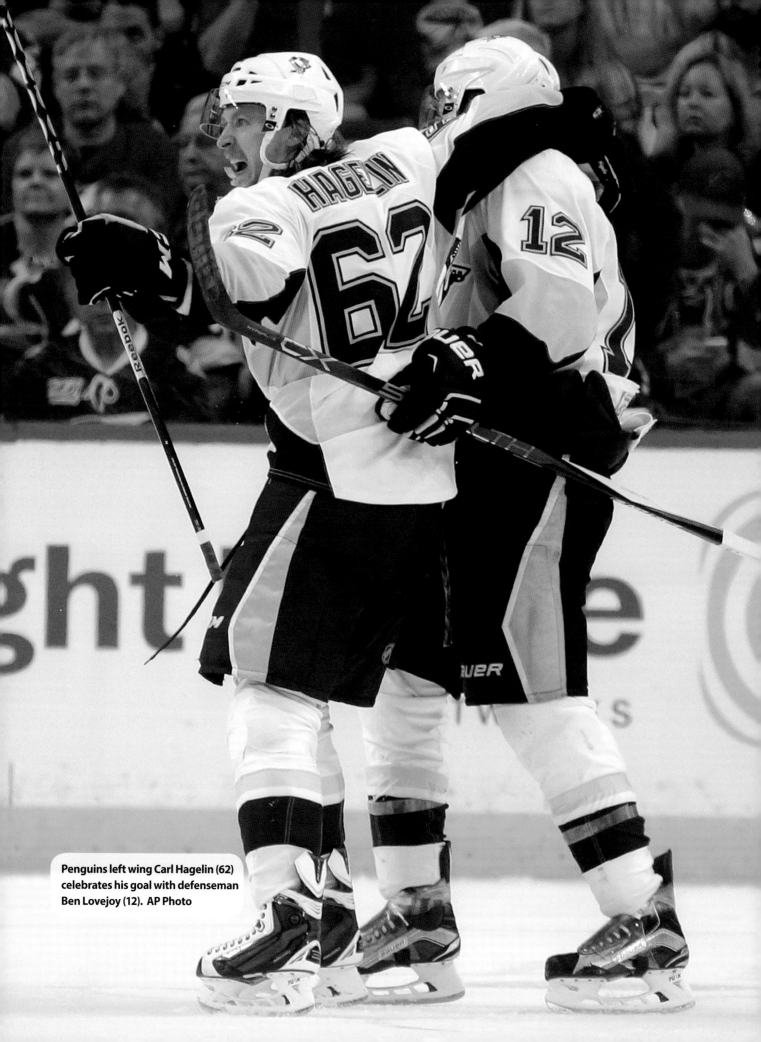

Penguins left wing Carl Hagelin (62) celebrates his goal with defenseman Ben Lovejoy (12). AP Photo

PENGUINS DOWN LIGHTNING FOR 2-1 SERIES LEAD

Penguins left wing Carl Hagelin (62) scores a goal against Lightning goalie Andrei Vasilevskiy. Penguins right wing Phil Kessel (81) got an assist on the play. AP Photo

Sidney Crosby, Phil Kessel and Chris Kunitz scored third-period goals to help the Pittsburgh Penguins beat the Tampa Bay Lightning 4-2 in Game 3 of the Eastern Conference finals.

Carl Hagelin snapped a scoreless tie late in the second period and Matt Murray had 26 saves for the Penguins, who took a 2-1 lead in the best-of-seven series and proved that they're far

Lightning goalie Andrei Vasilevskiy (88) looks back for the puck too late as Penguins right wing Phil Kessel (81) shoots and scores. AP Photo

from a one-man show.

"You don't win consistently without depth," Crosby said after scoring the winning goal for the second time in three nights.

Crosby's power-play goal off a pass from Evgeni Malkin restored a two-goal lead midway through the final period. Kunitz also beat goalie Andrei Vasilevskiy from the right circle to make it 4-1.

"It was a 4-on-3 so we had a one-timer on either side and [Malkin] was in a good spot to shoot it at the top of the ice," Crosby said. "He's just smart with the puck, and he's going to make the right decision. I don't think I called for it, but maybe I did."

Tyler Johnson and Ondrej Palat scored for the Lightning. They have lost two straight after winning the series opener in Pittsburgh. The

defending Eastern Conference champions were outshot 48-28, including 38-16 over the last two periods.

"Every team is good offensively when they play in their system," Pittsburgh defenseman Kris Letang said. "Our system is to play north-south and get the puck deep. When we do that, we have a good chance to win."

Vasilevskiy won Game 1 for the Lightning in relief of the injured Ben Bishop, and the Penguins took Game 2 in Pittsburgh when Crosby scored the first overtime playoff goal of his career less than a minute into the extra period.

The Lightning were outshot by a combined 76-41 in the first two games, but they weren't concerned with that disparity as much as by a lack of good scoring chances -- a problem they hoped to rectify by coming out more aggressive to try to put additional pressure on Penguins goalie Murray.

And for a while, they did.

Murray, though, had 12 saves in the opening period, but the Lightning couldn't keep up the pace. Pittsburgh controlled the puck for much of the second period, taking 21 shots to Tampa Bay's six and finally breaking through against the 21-year-old goaltender Vasilevskiy when Kessel chased down a loose puck before flicking a shot

from the right circle.

Vasilevskiy, who had stopped Kessel on a breakaway earlier in the period, blocked the shot directly toward Hagelin, who tipped it in with 10 seconds remaining before the second intermission.

"It was a great second period," Crosby said. "I thought we created a ton of chances, and to get one that late in the period felt good."

Kessel's team-leading seventh goal this postseason gave the Penguins a short-lived two-goal lead in the third period. Johnson countered for Tampa Bay just 14 seconds later, taking a pass from Nikita Kucherov and barreling in on Murray, who was unable to stop a shot that bounced off his upper body before continuing into the net.

Vasilevskiy, making his third career playoff start, finished with 44 saves. He has stopped 115 of 123 shots since taking over for Bishop during Game 1.

"Vasilevskiy has been excellent. He has really kept us in [the last two] games," Lightning defenseman Anton Stralman said.

The Lightning have lost consecutive games for the first time this postseason.

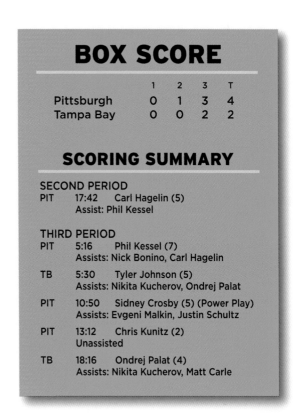

BOX SCORE

	1	2	3	T
Pittsburgh	0	1	3	4
Tampa Bay	0	0	2	2

SCORING SUMMARY

SECOND PERIOD
PIT   17:42   Carl Hagelin (5)
Assist: Phil Kessel

THIRD PERIOD
PIT   5:16   Phil Kessel (7)
Assists: Nick Bonino, Carl Hagelin

TB   5:30   Tyler Johnson (5)
Assists: Nikita Kucherov, Ondrej Palat

PIT   10:50   Sidney Crosby (5) (Power Play)
Assists: Evgeni Malkin, Justin Schultz

PIT   13:12   Chris Kunitz (2)
Unassisted

TB   18:16   Ondrej Palat (4)
Assists: Nikita Kucherov, Matt Carle

SIDNEY CROSBY

Sidney Crosby does not have an off switch. If there was one, Patric Hornqvist believes he would have found it by now.

Not once over the last two years while playing alongside one of the NHL's most popular players has Hornqvist seen an exasperated sigh, a roll of the eyes or so much as a smirk from the superstar who has dutifully served as one of the faces for the league from the moment the Pittsburgh Penguins drafted him No. 1 overall in 2005 and he became tasked with restoring the languishing franchise to glory.

"It's crazy how well-prepared he is for everything," Hornqvist said.

Of course it's easy to say now, with the Penguins back in the Stanley Cup Final. Their captain and two-time MVP seems restored to his place among the game's elite after ending a seven-year drought between appearances in the NHL's marquee event.

It's a gap few saw coming when the 21-year-old Crosby held the Cup aloft in joy in Detroit back in 2009 after beating the Red Wings in seven taut games.

"Everybody thought (we'd) win 5-6-7 in the next 10 years," said recently retired Pittsburgh forward Pascal Dupuis.

Everybody thought wrong. The burgeoning dynasty fizzled, with Crosby bearing the brunt of perpetual disappointment, accepting the blame for

Captain Sidney Crosby (87) moves the puck during first round playoff action. AP Photo

Crosby has been the driving force as the Penguins look to win their fourth Stanley Cup title. AP Photo

everything from his health to spotty goaltending to a top-heavy roster that lacked the depth necessary to make a deep postseason run.

"Look, this is his third final in his short career to this point, and that's pretty good," said former Pittsburgh coach Ed Olczyk, who coached Crosby as a rookie in 2005-06. "Now, in saying that, there haven't been many teams that have underachieved more than the Pittsburgh Penguins over the course of the last five or six years."

A label Crosby took personally even as circumstances — some beyond his control, some not — made him struggle to shed it.

"You just have to be able to put it all together at the right time," Crosby said. "I don't think we necessarily lacked those things in years we didn't win. I think you just have to be able to put it together and come up with those big plays at timely times."

And in some ways, Crosby had to grow up, too. For all his talent — he's never finished outside the top 10 in points per game in any season in which he's played enough games to qualify — he can

occasionally be too unselfish with the puck on his stick, sometimes trading wide-open shots for difficult passes in search of a teammate who may or may not be ready for them.

It's a line he's learned to straddle more carefully under Mike Sullivan, who freed Crosby from the constraints placed on him by former coach Mike Johnston. Sullivan encouraged Crosby to embrace his creativity so long as he finds a way to do it responsibly. It's not a coincidence that Crosby put up 31 goals and 36 assists in 52 games with Sullivan on the bench.

"He's a threat," Sullivan said. "Every time he jumps over the boards, we feel like he's a threat to score, just a threat as far as putting pressure on our opponent's defense. He has that twinkle in his eye, I think."

"Everything about him is about how he creates a competitive advantage for himself," Sullivan said. "Watching it every day I've grown to have more respect and more admiration for the type of effort he's put in to be the best player in the world."

The Penguins Chris Kunitz (14) and J.T. Brown (23) of the Lightning battle after the whistle. Both players were penalized and the teams played 4-on-4.
AP Photo

LIGHTNING HOLD OFF PENGUINS RALLY

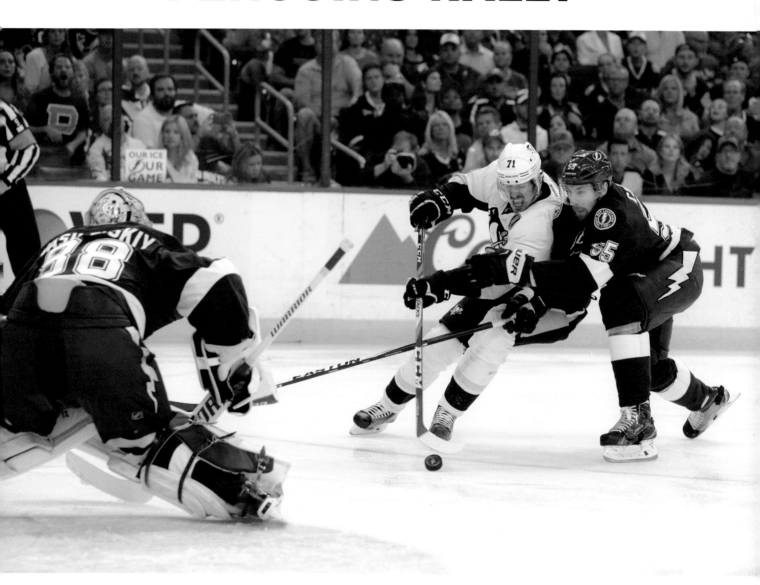

Penguins' Evgeni Malkin, center, tries for a shot on goal as Lightning goalie Andrei Vasilevskiy (88), and defenseman Braydon Coburn (55) defend. AP Photo

Ryan Callahan provided an early spark, Andrei Vasilevskiy made two big saves in the closing minutes to avoid a total third-period collapse, and the resilient Tampa Bay Lightning held on for a 4-3 victory over the Pittsburgh Penguins in Game 4 of the Eastern Conference finals.

Callahan tipped a shot past goalie Matt

Penguins goalie Marc-Andre Fleury (29) eyes a shot by Lightning center Cedric Paquette (13). **AP Photo**

Murray just 17 seconds into the game. Andrej Sustr, Jonathan Drouin and Tyler Johnson also scored and the Lightning rebounded after being badly outplayed in the previous two games to even the series 2-2 heading back to Pittsburgh for Game 5.

"It doesn't matter how you get there," Lightning coach Jon Cooper said after the Penguins scored three times in 12 minutes to turn a potential rout into a nail-biter.

"Whether you're up 4-0 and it becomes 4-3, or you're down 3-0 and it becomes 4-3, it doesn't matter. The goal is to win the hockey game," the

coach added.

"When you wake up in the morning, it's not how they came back and made it a game. It's that the series is 2-2."

Vasilevskiy had a 4-0 lead entering the third period, but the Penguins didn't give up. Phil Kessel and Evgeni Malkin scored to give Pittsburgh hope, and Chris Kunitz's power-play goal trimmed the deficit to one with a little less than 7 minutes remaining.

"We were not the more determined team for the first half of the game," Penguins coach Mike Sullivan said. "They are a good team, and we

knew this was going to be a hard game."

Tampa Bay was outshot 16-7 over the final 20 minutes after dominating the first two periods. Malkin and Jason Schultz tested Vasilevskiy in the final 2:10, but Vasilevskiy stopped both efforts to tie the score.

The 21-year-old goaltender, filling in for injured Vezina Trophy finalist Ben Bishop, finished with 35 saves in his fourth career playoff start.

Marc-Andre Fleury replaced Murray in goal for the Penguins at the start of the third, and Kessel's team-leading eighth goal began the rally that just fell short.

The Lightning were outshot 89-49 in the previous two games, a disparity that Cooper called "unacceptable" after the Penguins took a 2-1 series lead.

But the experience of the highs of lows of last year's playoff run to the Stanley Cup final has served the defending conference champions well over the past month.

While acknowledging there was a sense of urgency to play better, Cooper and his players insisted the team was not overly discouraged after being badly outplayed in Games 2 and 3 because they been down in series before and found ways to come back.

The Penguins, relentless in Game 3 when they took 48 shots en route to a 4-2 victory, were unable to convert a couple of good scoring chances in the first period and had limited opportunities until finally cracking Vasilevskiy in the third.

Kessel scored at 1:18 of the third period, beating Vasilevskiy from above the right circle. The goal was his team-leading eighth of the playoffs, with Nick Bonino and Brian Dumoulin picking up assists.

Malkin scored at 11:13 and the Penguins drew closer when Kunitz added his goal with 6:52 remaining.

Penguins captain Sidney Crosby said the slow start was not as "horrible as it was made out to be," noting Tampa Bay entered the night as the more desperate team after losing two straight.

"It wasn't the start we wanted for sure," Crosby said, "but we still had our chances to get back into the game before it became 4-0."

BOX SCORE

	1	2	3	T
Pittsburgh	0	0	3	3
Tampa Bay	2	2	0	4

SCORING SUMMARY

FIRST PERIOD
TB   0:27   Ryan Callahan (2)
      Assists: Victor Hedman, J.T. Brown

TB   14:28   Andrej Sustr (1)
      Assists: Nikita Kucherov, Alex Killorn

SECOND PERIOD
TB   14:38   Jonathan Drouin (4) (Power Play)
      Assists: Ondrej Palat, Victor Hedman

TB   17:48   Tyler Johnson (6)
      Assists: Nikita Kucherov, Alex Killorn

THIRD PERIOD
PIT   1:18   Phil Kessel (8)
      Assists: Nick Bonino, Brian Dumoulin

PIT   11:13   Evgeni Malkin (4)
      Assist: Ian Cole

PIT   13:08   Chris Kunitz (3) (Power Play)
      Assists: Justin Schultz, Conor Sheary

Tampa Bay Lightning's Nikita Kucherov (86), top, brings the puck around the goal to score on Penguins goalie Marc-Andre Fleury (29).
AP Photo

CONFERENCE FINALS MAY 22, 2016 CONSOL ENERGY CENTER PITTSBURGH, PENNSYLVANIA

PITTSBURGH PENGUINS 3 ● TAMPA BAY LIGHTNING 4

JOHNSON'S OT GOAL GIVES LIGHTNING GAME 5 WIN

Lightning center Tyler Johnson (9) celebrates his game winning goal as the puck kicks out of the net behind Penguins goalie Marc-Andre Fleury. **AP Photo**

Tyler Johnson didn't even feel it. Lightning teammate Jason Garrison's wrister smacked off Johnson's back and into the Pittsburgh Penguins net 53 seconds into overtime, giving Tampa Bay a 4-3 victory and a 3-2 lead in the best-of-seven series. A year after falling to the Chicago Blackhawks in the Cup finals, Tampa Bay can head back to the championship round with a win in Game 6.

"I was just battling in front," Johnson said. "I saw Garry starting to shoot it, thought he was going for my head again, so I turned around."

Just in time for his seventh -- and most important -- goal of the playoffs. The Lightning are 12-1 in the last 13 postseason games in which Johnson has scored.

"He's a winner, that's what winners do," Tampa Bay coach Jon Cooper said of Johnson. "They don't back down."

Even on the road. Even down a pair of goals. Even trailing by one heading into the third period against a team that began the night 46-0 on the season when leading after two. Yet Tampa Bay survived by consistently and expertly counterpunching every time the Penguins provided an opportunity.

Nikita Kucherov scored twice -- including a wraparound that beat Marc-Andre Fleury and tied it at 3 with just 3:16 left in regulation. Alex Killorn picked up his fifth of the playoffs as the Lightning handed the Penguins consecutive losses for the first time since January. Andrei Vasilevskiy stopped 31 shots to outplay Fleury, who returned to the lineup for the first time in more than seven weeks.

Fleury finished with 21 saves, but couldn't protect leads of 2-0 and 3-2.

"It wasn't the best I have felt in a game," Fleury said. "Still, I have been practicing a lot, so I should have been better."

Brian Dumoulin, Chris Kunitz and Patric Hornqvist scored for the Penguins, who appeared to be in firm control at certain points only to find themselves on the brink of elimination.

"This is the first time we've been in this position," coach Mike Sullivan said. "I know our guys will respond the right way. They have for four, five months now."

If the Penguins want to play at least one more game in Pittsburgh this season, they don't really have a choice. While the Penguins have peppered Vasilevskiy for the better part of five games, the Lightning keep finding ways to create quality chances around the Pittsburgh net, though Garrison's flick toward Johnson might not exactly qualify.

BOX SCORE

	1	2	3	OT	T
Pittsburgh	1	2	0	0	3
Tampa Bay	0	2	1	1	4

SCORING SUMMARY

FIRST PERIOD
PIT   19:59   Brian Dumoulin (1)
          Assists: Bryan Rust, Chris Kunitz

SECOND PERIOD
PIT   1:30   Patric Hornqvist (7)
          Assists: Carl Hagelin, Olli Maatta

TB   13:15   Alex Killorn (5)
          Assist: Andrej Sustr

TB   14:25   Nikita Kucherov (10)
          Assist: Vladislav Namestnikov

PIT   19:10   Chris Kunitz (4)
          Assists: Evgeni Malkin, Olli Maatta

THIRD PERIOD
TB   16:44   Nikita Kucherov (11)
          Assists: Tyler Johnson, Ondrej Palat

OVERTIME
TB   0:53   Tyler Johnson (7)
          Assists: Jason Garrison, Nikita Kucherov

Penguins Sidney Crosby (87) has his shot deflected in front of Lightning goalie Andrei Vasilevskiy (88). AP Photo

"No shot's a bad shot in overtime," Garrison said with a laugh.

Back in his customary starting spot for the first time in 52 days after dealing with a concussion that coincided with the rise of rookie Matt Murray, Fleury appeared to be plenty fresh. He sprinted in full gear onto the Consol Energy Center ice for his 100th career playoff appearance and looked fine while making a split save on Johnson in the second period that few of his brethren can pull off. He was helped by teammates more than willing to get on their bellies. The Penguins blocked 22 shots before they even made it to the goal crease and continued their series-long dominance in creating pressure at the other end.

Dumoulin's first goal in 17 months in the final second of the first period put Pittsburgh in front. Hornqvist's tap-in off Carl Hagelin's feed made it 2-0 just 90 seconds into the second.

Sidney Crosby (87) and Phil Kessel (81) celebrate Crosby's second period goal. AP Photo

STAYIN' ALIVE
PENGUINS FORCE GAME 7

Penguins Sidney Crosby (87) beats Lightning defensemen Anton Stralman (6) en route to his second period goal. AP Photo

The Pittsburgh Penguins made good on Evgeni Malkin's pledge to force Game 7 in the Eastern Conference final.

Sidney Crosby had a goal and an assist, and Phil Kessel, Kris Letang, Bryan Rust and Nick Bonino also scored in a 5-2 victory that evened the best-of-seven series with the Tampa Bay Lightning 3-3.

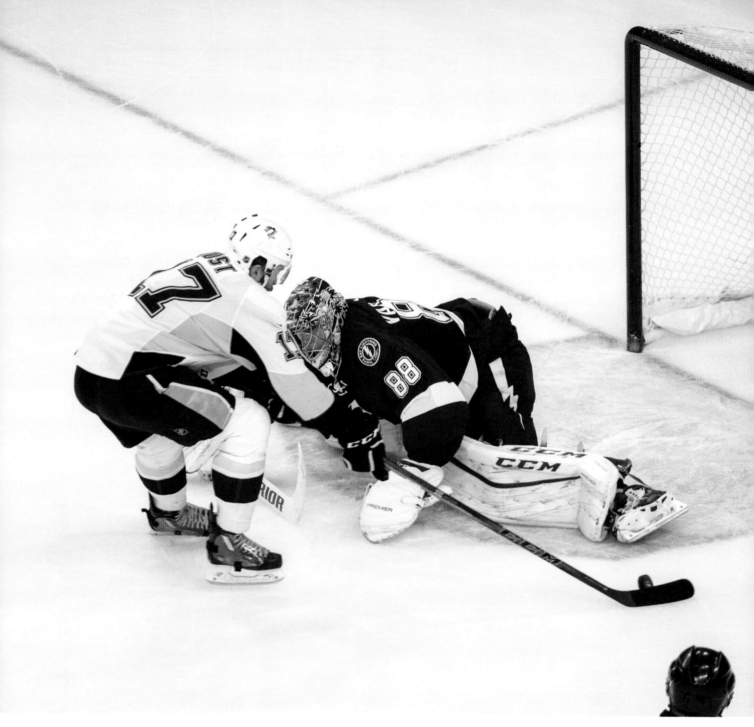

Penguins Bryan Rust (17) dekes around Lightning goalie Andrei Vasilevskiy (88) to score. AP Photo

Game 7 will have the Penguins hoping to reach the Stanley Cup Final for the first time since 2009 and the Lightning looking to advance to the Cup Final for the second straight year.

"I just told them to embrace the moment," Pittsburgh coach Mike Sullivan said. "It's a great opportunity for us. These are the type of circumstances to where you have an opportunity to write your own story.

"They had a certain mindset going into this game: 'We're going to leave it all out there and do everything we can to bring this back to Pittsburgh.' And, certainly that's what they did."

Malkin was the most demonstrative of the players expressing confidence the Penguins could take the series back to Pittsburgh, saying he believed in himself and his teammates and that they could return home for a seventh game "for sure."

Crosby stepped up with his third game-winning goal of the series. The Penguins captain assisted on Kessel's 5-on-3 power-play goal in the opening period and later skated around Tampa Bay defenseman Anton Stralman into the clear before sending a wrist shot between goalie Andrei Vasilevskiy's legs for a 3-0 lead in the final minute of the second period.

"We know the circumstances," Crosby said. "It makes you go out there with a mindset of playing desperate. I think we had confidence in the whole group. I think everyone played great.

"Everyone contributed in their own way. In a big game like this you, don't do anything special, just do your job. I think that's gotten us this far."

Rookie goaltender Matt Murray returned to the lineup after being replaced as the starter for Game 5 by Marc-Andre Fleury, but his 10th playoff victory did not come without a bit of suspense.

Brian Boyle scored twice in the third period for Tampa Bay, with one of the goals bouncing off Kessel before getting past Murray, who finished with 28 saves. The second score drew the Lightning within one goal with 7:17 remaining.

Instead of flinching, Murray, who turns 22 on Wednesday, kept his composure down the stretch to help the Penguins avoid relinquishing a third-period lead for the second straight game.

"I just think it's part of his DNA," Sullivan said. "He has a calming influence. He doesn't get rattled if he lets a goal in. He continues to compete.

"That's usually an attribute that takes years to acquire. And to have it at such a young age is impressive. I think one of his biggest strengths is just his ability to stay in the moment."

Rust's breakaway goal at 17:52 of the third gave Pittsburgh breathing room, and Bonino added an empty-netter to finish it off.

"We had a great chance tonight and just tip-toed around a little bit," Boyle said. "We were tentative and weren't aggressive."

Kessel's goal was his team-leading ninth of the playoffs. Crosby had the primary assist, his first point since delivering game-winners in Games 2 and 3, and Malkin also had an assist to extend his point streak to four games after a slow start in the series.

BOX SCORE

	1	2	3	T
Pittsburgh	1	2	2	5
Tampa Bay	0	0	2	2

SCORING SUMMARY

FIRST PERIOD
PIT   18:46   Phil Kessel (9) (Power Play)
        Assists: Sidney Crosby, Evgeni Malkin

SECOND PERIOD
PIT   7:40   Kris Letang (2)
        Assists: Conor Sheary, Nick Bonino

PIT   19:34   Sidney Crosby (6)
        Assist: Patric Hornqvist

THIRD PERIOD
TB   5:30   Brian Boyle (4)
        Unassisted

TB   12:43   Brian Boyle (5)
        Assists: Slater Koekkoek, Jonathan Drouin

PIT   17:52   Bryan Rust (3)
        Assists: Chris Kunitz, Olli Maatta

PIT   19:06   Nick Bonino (3)
        Assist: Ben Lovejoy

Penguins Bryan Rust (17) celebrates scoring the game winner on Lightning goalie Andrei Vasilevskiy during the second period. AP Photo

PENGUINS HEADING BACK TO STANLEY CUP

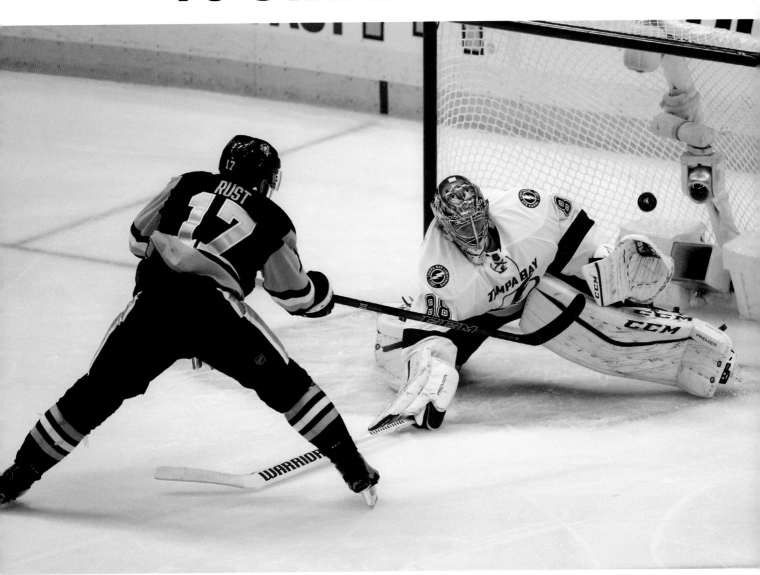

Penguins Bryan Rust (17) shoots and scores his first goal of the night against Lightning goalie Andrei Vasilevskiy. AP Photo

Pittsburgh Penguins rookie forward Bryan Rust, who began training camp hoping just to make the team, scored both of Pittsburgh's goals as the Penguins sent the Tampa Bay Lightning home following their 2-1 win in Game 7 of the Eastern Conference finals.

In a building littered with stars, it was the relentlessness of the 24-year-old Rust and the

Penguins goalie Matt Murray (30) covers up the rebound on a shot by Lightning center Steven Stamkos. AP Photo

steadiness of 22-year-old goaltender Matt Murray that provided the difference as the Penguins reached the finals for the first time since 2009.

"I'm in that mode where I'm getting the bounces and the breaks right now," Rust said.

Ones Rust and his teammates are earning. The Penguins rallied from a 3-2 deficit by controlling the final two games of the best-of-seven series, winning 5-2 in Tampa Bay in Game 6, then backing it up with what coach Mike Sullivan said "might

have been the most complete 60-minute effort we had."

In disarray in December when Sullivan took over for Mike Johnston, the Penguins have sprinted through April and May and will head into June with a chance to win the franchise's fourth Cup, one that would serve as a bookend to its last triumph seven years ago when stars Sidney Crosby and Evgeni Malkin were still in their early 20s.

They're older now. Wiser. And undaunted by a series of postseason failures that made it seem like the window of their primes was closing. Yet here they are after dispatching the New York Rangers in five games, the Presidents' Trophy-winning Washington Capitals in six and the defending Eastern Conference champion Lightning in seven.

"They played better hockey than us the whole series," said Tampa Bay defenseman Anton Stralman.

Jonathan Drouin scored his fifth goal of the playoffs for the Lightning and Andrei Vasilevskiy made 37 saves, but it wasn't enough to send Tampa Bay back to the Cup finals for a second straight year. Captain Steven Stamkos had two shots in 11:55 in his return from a two-month layoff while dealing with blood clots, his best chance coming on a breakaway in the second period that deflected off Murray and trickled wide.

"I thought I beat him," Stamkos said. "It just went through him and out the other side. It was close, but we didn't generate enough offensively in order to win a game."

Mostly because the Penguins didn't let them. It's part of what Sullivan calls "playing the right way," a way abetted by the influx of speed brought in by general manager Jim Rutherford. That group includes Rust, who forced his way onto the roster thanks to feverish skating and a self-confidence that belies his nondescript 5-foot-11 frame.

That effort -- or "desperation level," as Crosby calls it -- provided the Penguins with the boost they needed to overcome a bit of unfortunate history and the return of Stamkos. Pittsburgh had dropped five straight Game 7s at home, including a 1-0 loss to Tampa Bay in 2011 in a series both Crosby and Malkin missed due to injury.

That loss had become symbolic of the franchise's postseason shortcomings following that gritty run to the Cup in 2009 that culminated with a Game 7 win in Detroit that was supposed to be the launching pad of a dynasty.

Seven long years later, with an entirely new cast around mainstays Crosby, Malkin, Kris Letang, Chris Kunitz and Marc-Andre Fleury, the Penguins have returned to the league's biggest stage.

"We've always believed in one another," Crosby said. "Trying to get back, it's not easy."

Not by a long shot.

"The biggest challenge is ahead of us," Crosby said. "We have to finish it off the right way."

BOX SCORE

	1	2	3	T
Pittsburgh	0	2	0	2
Tampa Bay	0	1	0	1

SCORING SUMMARY

SECOND PERIOD

PIT   1:55   Bryan Rust (4)
Assists: Chris Kunitz, Evgeni Malkin

TB   9:36   Jonathan Drouin (5)
Assists: Valtteri Filppula, Victor Hedman

PIT   10:06   Bryan Rust (5)
Assists: Ben Lovejoy, Evgeni Malkin

The Penguins celebrate their 2-1 win over the Lightning to advance to the Stanley Cup Finals. Inset: Sidney Crosby (87), left wing Chris Kunitz (14) and center Evgeni Malkin (71) hold the Prince of Wales Trophy. AP Photo

COACH MIKE SULLIVAN

Mike Sullivan had a clear vision for the Pittsburgh Penguins when he was hired as the team's new head coach in December.

The former Boston Bruins head coach and a long-time assistant to John Tortorella in Tampa, New York and Vancouver, Sullivan wanted to play to the strengths of Sidney Crosby, Kris Letang and the rest of the team's best players when he replaced the fired Mike Johnston.

"And when you look at our core players they all want to play a speed game," Sullivan said. "Speed in all of its forms, whether it's foot speed or team speed — your ability to move the puck and change the point of attack quickly to create opportunity or to create a competitive advantage — is what I envisioned with this group.

"And so we've tried to implement some strategies to give these players an opportunity to play to their strengths."

It's been a rousing success with the Penguins not only racing to one of the NHL's best records from the point of his hiring, but the club's first Stanley Cup final appearance since 2009.

The numbers before and after Sullivan's promotion from the team's AHL affiliate in Wilkes-Barre are jarring.

Scoring skyrocketed, from a mediocre 2.36 goals per game under Johnston to 3.24 per game under Sullivan, a number that would have led

Penguins head coach Mike Sullivan talks strategy with Sidney Crosby (87). AP Photo

Penguins head coach Mike Sullivan sets up a play during a timeout in a recent playoff game. AP Photo

the league this season. Not only were they finding the net more often, but controlling the puck with increased frequency and by a wide margin. The Penguins boasted a conference-leading 55.4 per cent puck possession mark after Sullivan took over, well above the sluggish rate under Johnston.

Outshot slightly before the coaching change, the Penguins badly outshot teams under the new head coach, averaging close to six more shots per game than their opponent.

As for those core players Sullivan wanted to unlock, they surged as well, notably Crosby who had 30 goals and 66 points in 52 games and Letang who posted 15 goals and 53 points in 46 games.

Speed was apparent on all four lines of the Pittsburgh lineup as well as on a defense that moved the puck quickly up the ice.

It was an evolution that saw the eventual Eastern Conference champions become a high-scoring, puck-hogging juggernaut.

The first thing Crosby noticed about his new coach when he took over Dec. 12 was his propensity for details as well as the clarity of his expectations, both for how the team and individuals were to play.

"That was very clear right off the bat so I think as a player the direction that he wanted the team to play and everything that came along with that, I think was well-understood and well-received," Crosby said. "He was going to hold everyone accountable no matter what position or what the detail was. Everything was important."

That accountability was appreciated beyond the stars.

"He doesn't let anyone off the hook as far as making plays, turning pucks over, which I think, that accountability is really good for us," said defenseman Ian Cole.

STANLEY CUP CHAMPIONS

Penguins fans gather outside Consol Energy Arena prior to Game 1 of the Stanley Cup. AP Photo

Penguins center Nick Bonino (13) celebrates his game winning goal with right wing Phil Kessel (81). AP Photo

STANLEY CUP FINALS

MAY 30, 2016 CONSOL ENERGY CENTER PITTSBURGH, PENNSYLVANIA

PITTSBURGH PENGUINS 3 • SAN JOSE SHARKS 2

PENGUINS EDGE SHARKS IN GAME 1

Penguins center Nick Bonino (13) scores the winning goal over Sharks goalie Martin Jones' (31) right shoulder. AP Photo

Nick Bonino darted to the net and knocked in Kris Letang's centering pass with 2:33 remaining, lifting the Pittsburgh Penguins to a 3-2 victory over the San Jose Sharks in Game 1 of the Stanley Cup finals.

Pittsburgh recovered after blowing an early two-goal lead and spoiled San Jose's long-awaited debut on the league's biggest stage.

Penguins Conor Sheary (43) watches his shot sail past Sharks goalie Martin Jones (31) for a goal during the first period. **AP Photo**

Letang and Carl Hagelin took turns digging the puck out of the corner behind the San Jose net when Letang emerged with it and slipped it to Bonino, who collected himself and flicked it past Martin Jones' blocker for his fourth goal of the playoffs.

"Tanger put it right on my stick," Bonino said. "It was a shot that wasn't my hardest shot by any means but I kind of found a way to flip it over him."

Bonino has spent much of the past two months as the heady, understated center on Pittsburgh's hottest line while playing between hard-shooting Phil Kessel and Hagelin. Dubbed "HBK" -- a chant that occasionally greets them when they flip over the boards and onto the ice

-- they have powered the Penguins to their first Cup finals in seven years. Yet it was Bonino, whose hockey IQ is considered his greatest attribute by Pittsburgh coach Mike Sullivan, who scored the group's biggest goal of the postseason.

"He does all the things right and found himself in a great position and capitalized on it," Pittsburgh forward Chris Kunitz said.

Rookies Bryan Rust and Conor Sheary also scored for the Penguins, though Rust left in the third period after absorbing a shot to the head from San Jose's Patrick Marleau. Matt Murray -- who like Rust and Sheary spent a significant amount of time this season with the team's American Hockey League affiliate in Wilkes-Barre/Scranton -- finished with 24 saves.

Jones made 38 stops but couldn't get over in time on Bonino's knuckler. The Penguins threw 41 shots at Jones, the most he has faced in a regulation game during the playoffs. The Sharks spent a large portion of the third period on their heels and their dynamic power play failed to record a single shot when Ben Lovejoy went to the penalty box with 2:09 to play.

"They played their game for longer stretches than we did and that's what happens," San Jose coach Peter DeBoer said.

The Sharks looked a step slow -- maybe two steps slow -- while searching for their footing early on against the Penguins.

Rust gave the Penguins the lead 12:46 into the first when he slammed home a rebound off a Justin Schultz shot for his sixth of the postseason, a franchise record for playoff goals by a rookie.

Less than a minute later, Sheary, who didn't become a regular until the middle of January, made it 2-0 when Sidney Crosby whipped a blind backhand cross-ice pass to Sheary's stick. Sheary's wrist shot from the right circle zipped by Jones, and the Penguins appeared to be in complete command by overwhelming the Sharks in a way few have in months.

San Jose regained its composure during the first intermission and responded with a big surge. Tomas Hertl jammed a power-play shot from just outside the crease between Murray's legs 3:02 into the second to give the Sharks momentum. Late in the second, Marleau collected a rebound off a Brent Burns one-timer behind the Pittsburgh net and then beat Murray on a wraparound that caromed off Murray's extended right leg and into the net.

Yet Bonino, who arrived in an offseason trade with Vancouver, helped the Penguins improve to 9-3 at home all-time in the Cup final by sliding to a familiar spot in search of a familiar result.

BOX SCORE

	1	2	3	T
Pittsburgh	2	0	1	3
San Jose	0	2	0	2

SCORING SUMMARY

FIRST PERIOD
PIT   12:46   Bryan Rust (6)
Assists: Justin Schultz, Chris Kunitz

PIT   13:48   Conor Sheary (3)
Assists: Sidney Crosby, Olli Maatta

SECOND PERIOD
SJ   3:02   Tomas Hertl (6) (Power Play)
Assists: Joonas Donskoi, Brent Burns

SJ   18:12   Patrick Marleau (5)
Assists: Brent Burns, Logan Couture

THIRD PERIOD
PIT   17:27   Nick Bonino (4)
Assists: Kris Letang, Carl Hagelin

Penguins goalie Matt Murray (30) stops a shot by the Sharks Nick Spaling (16) during the first period. AP Photo

SHEARY'S OT GOAL GIVES PENGUINS 2-0 SERIES LEAD

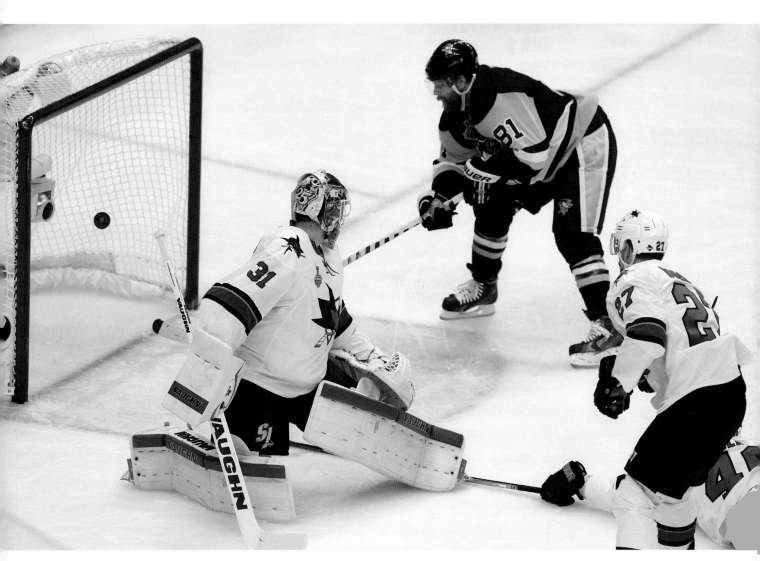

Phil Kessel (81) gives the Penguins a 1-0 lead in the second period. AP Photo

Sidney Crosby always enters the faceoff circle with a plan in mind.

And every once in a while the plan in the Pittsburgh superstars head morphs into reality. Such was the case during overtime in Game 2 of the Stanley Cup finals.

Crosby's faceoff win helped set up Conor Sheary's perfectly placed wrist shot 2:35 into overtime, one that lifted the Penguins to a 2-1 victory over the San Jose Sharks and a 2-0 lead in the best-of-seven series.

"I call 25 faceoffs a night," Crosby said with a laugh. "I got 24 wrong tonight."

It's the one Crosby got right that will live on if the Penguins find a way to close out their fourth championship. Just before heading to the dot to the right of San Jose goalie Martin Jones, Crosby told Sheary to line up on the wall and then look for a soft spot in the San Jose defense.

Crosby won the draw and dropped it to defenseman Kris Letang, who feigned a shot then slipped it to Sheary. The 23-year-old rookie zipped it over Jones' outstretched glove for his fourth goal of the playoffs and second of the series.

"It's pretty surreal," said Sheary, who began the season in the minor leagues.

Sharks defenseman Justin Braun tied it with 4:05 left in regulation, but San Jose fell to 0-4 when pushed to overtime in the playoffs after getting largely outplayed for much of the night by the quicker, more nimble Penguins.

Phil Kessel scored his 10th goal of the postseason for Pittsburgh, and Matt Murray made 21 stops. The Penguins have not trailed at any point while reeling off four straight playoff victories after falling behind in the Eastern Conference final against Tampa Bay.

"Game 1 was decided in last two minutes, tonight was decided in overtime," Sharks coach Peter DeBoer said. "We'll hold off on the funeral."

Maybe, but time is running out. Only five teams in NHL history have come back from a 2-0 deficit in the final to win the Cup.

While the Sharks were better in Game 2, the sustained push the Penguins were expecting from the Western Conference champions failed to materialize until it was nearly too late. Pittsburgh did the two things that have been the club's hallmark since coach Mike Sullivan took over for Mike Johnston in mid-December, controlling the puck and forcing the San Jose to go a full 200 feet to create chances.

Pittsburgh's forecheck made San Jose labor just to get the puck in the offensive zone and once there, the Penguins kept throwing black-and-gold clad bodies in the way.

Still, it took time for Pittsburgh's heady and hectic play to translate into a goal, with the group that's been Pittsburgh's best line for the last three months finally breaking through against Jones just before the midway point.

Thrust together as an experiment when Evgeni Malkin went out with a left elbow injury in mid-February, the trio of Kessel, Carl Hagelin and Nick Bonino have rapidly evolved into Pittsburgh's most dangerous line. They began the night with 90 combined points in 34 games, and added to it during another typically aggressive shift when Hagelin

BOX SCORE

	1	2	3	OT	T
Pittsburgh	0	1	0	1	2
San Jose	0	0	1	0	1

SCORING SUMMARY

SECOND PERIOD
PIT   8:20   Phil Kessel (10)
        Assists: Nick Bonino, Carl Hagelin

THIRD PERIOD
SJ   15:55   Justin Braun (1)
        Assists: Logan Couture, Joel Ward

OVERTIME
PIT   2:35   Conor Sheary (4)
        Assists: Kris Letang, Sidney Crosby

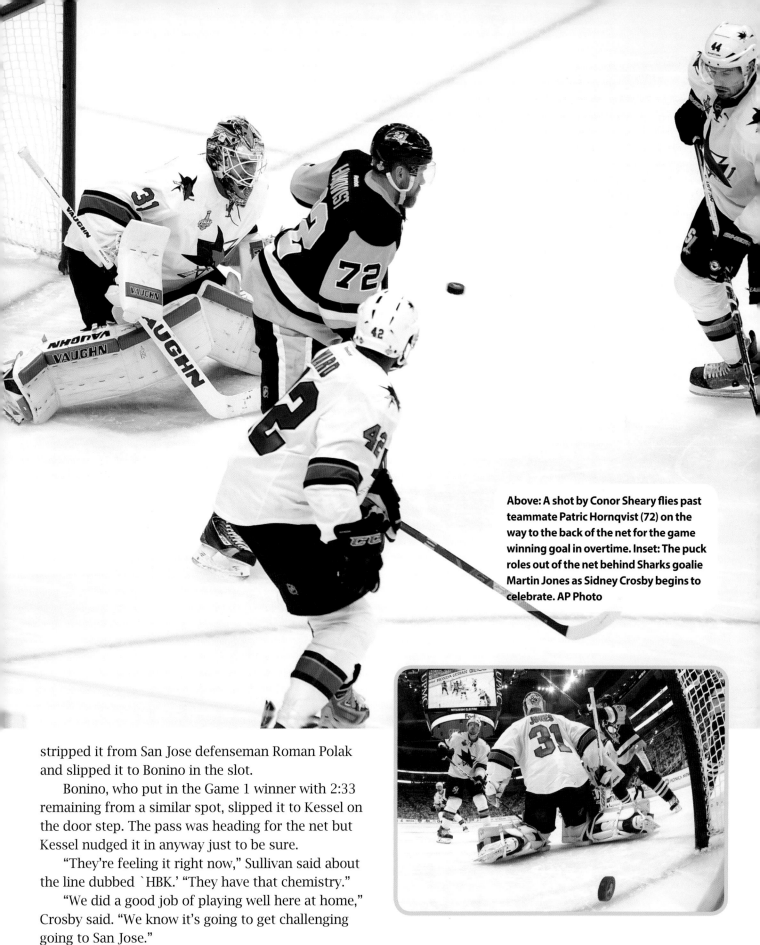

Above: A shot by Conor Sheary flies past teammate Patric Hornqvist (72) on the way to the back of the net for the game winning goal in overtime. Inset: The puck roles out of the net behind Sharks goalie Martin Jones as Sidney Crosby begins to celebrate. AP Photo

stripped it from San Jose defenseman Roman Polak and slipped it to Bonino in the slot.

Bonino, who put in the Game 1 winner with 2:33 remaining from a similar spot, slipped it to Kessel on the door step. The pass was heading for the net but Kessel nudged it in anyway just to be sure.

"They're feeling it right now," Sullivan said about the line dubbed `HBK.' "They have that chemistry."

"We did a good job of playing well here at home," Crosby said. "We know it's going to get challenging going to San Jose."

Sharks right wing Joonas Donskoi, center, celebrates with teammates after scoring the winning goal during overtime.
AP Photo

JUNE 4, 2016 SAP CENTER SAN JOSE, CALIFORNIA

PITTSBURGH PENGUINS 2 • SAN JOSE SHARKS 3

DONSKOI'S OT GOAL GIVES SAN JOSE LIFE IN CUP FINALS

Sharks right wing Joonas Donskoi (27), shoots and scores on a tough angle to give the San Jose their first ever Stanley Cup victory.
AP Photo

It took an extra 12 minutes 18 seconds of overtime and a nifty goal by the rookie Joonas Donskoi, but home ice turned out to be exactly what the San Jose Sharks needed as they came from behind for a 3-2 victory over the Pittsburgh Penguins in Game 3 of the Stanley Cup finals.

The victory was the Sharks' first in the series after they had dropped two games in Pittsburgh, and there had to be a collective sigh of relief when Donskoi skated from behind the net to fire the puck over the shoulder of Penguins goalie Matthew Murray. With the win, the Sharks avoided falling into a three-games-to-none hole in their first Cup finals appearance in their 24-year history.

They also picked up some much-needed confidence heading into Game 4.

"It's big," the Sharks' Joe Thornton said of the win. "We haven't had the lead too much in this series. To win this one, it's a huge confidence booster, and now we just need to continue it in Game 4."

Donskoi, 24, may have scored the most significant goal in franchise history, keeping San Jose's hopes of a Stanley Cup alive.

"I think I've had a lot of scoring chances through the whole finals," Donskoi said of the goal, his first of the series and his sixth of the postseason. "It was a good time to get it in."

The Sharks entered the third period trailing by 2-1 after the Penguins had sandwiched goals by Ben Lovejoy and Patric Hornqvist around one by San Jose's Justin Braun.

BOX SCORE

	1	2	3	OT	T
Pittsburgh	1	1	0	0	2
San Jose	1	0	1	1	3

SCORING SUMMARY

FIRST PERIOD
PIT   5:29   Ben Lovejoy (2)
Unassisted

SJ   9:34   Justin Braun (2)
Assists: Joe Thornton, Marc-Edouard Vlasic

SECOND PERIOD
PIT   19:07   Patric Hornqvist (8)
Assists: Ben Lovejoy, Olli Maatta

THIRD PERIOD
SJ   8:48   Joel Ward (7)
Assists: Joonas Donskoi, Joe Thornton

OVERTIME
SJ   12:18   Joonas Donskoi (6)
Assist: Chris Tierney

A high-sticking penalty against the Penguins' Nick Bonino gave the Sharks a four-minute power play, and they needed every second of it before Joel Ward fired a 41-foot slap shot that found a small opening between Murray's glove and left leg pad at 8:48.

The Sharks had hoped that the shift back to their home ice might provide the edge to help them counter the speed and opportunistic goals that had given the Penguins the first two games in the best-of-seven series.

San Jose did seem to feed off the home crowd early on, but the Penguins took a 1-0 lead at 5:29 of the first period when giveaways by goalie Martin Jones and defenseman Roman Polak put the puck on Lovejoy's stick, and his shot from the left point deflected off Polak and into the net.

San Jose tied the score a little more than four minutes later when Thornton found Braun unchecked just inside the blue line and his shot sailed past the screened Murray.

The Sharks dominated play throughout the second period, but Murray came up big with saves on tight shots by Brent Burns and Joel Ward, while Ward's linemate Logan Couture rang a wrist shot off the far post.

Defenseman Ben Lovejoy (12) celebrates with teammates after giving the Penguins a 1-0 lead in the first period. AP Photo

The Penguins took a 2-1 lead 53 seconds before the second period ended when Thornton lost the puck to Olli Maatta, who fed it to Lovejoy for a shot that deflected off Patric Hornqvist's stick and into the net.

But Jones said the thought of falling behind by three games to none had not rattled him.

"It's easy to stay focused in those moments," said Jones, who finished with 40 saves and made his biggest stop at 4:05 of overtime on a deflection by Bonino. "It was a must-win for us, and we got a better effort out of everyone tonight."

Despite his team's loss, Murray did not seemed discouraged.

"It's one game," he said. "It's a seven-game series. It's all about the next game. I think we outplayed them again today. We were the better team. I think we're in a good spot here heading forward."

Penguins Ian Cole (28) drills a shot that sails past Sharks goalie Martin Jones for a first period goal. Inset: Kris Letang (58) celebrates with Cole. AP Photo

STANLEY CUP FINALS

JUNE 6, 2016 · SAP CENTER · SAN JOSE, CALIFORNIA

PITTSBURGH PENGUINS 3 ● SAN JOSE SHARKS 1

PENS ON BRINK OF STANLEY CUP AFTER GAME 4 VICTORY

Penguins goalie Matt Murray stops a breakaway shot by Sharks center Patrick Marleau (12) during the second period. **AP Photo**

The Pittsburgh Penguins were confident that three straight games without a point for Evgeni Malkin and a rare off night by Matt Murray were an aberration more than a concern.

Bounce-back performances from those two key players moved the Penguins to the brink of winning the Stanley Cup.

Malkin scored one goal and assisted on another, Murray made 23 saves and the Penguins took a 3-1 series lead in the Stanley Cup finals by beating the San Jose Sharks 3-1 in Game 4.

"He's a world class player," Penguins

Penguins Evgeni Malkin, right, celebrates his second period goal. AP Photo

defenseman Ian Cole said of Malkin. "He's been going through a rough stretch. He's been really contributing in other ways than on the scoresheet. But obviously you saw how good he is today."

Malkin helped set up Cole's goal to open the scoring, then added one of his own on the power play to give Murray all the support needed.

Eric Fehr sealed it with a late goal after San Jose made a strong push in the third.

Two nights after allowing a soft game-tying goal to Joel Ward, Murray was steady throughout to put the Penguins one win from skating off with their fourth Stanley Cup in franchise history. They can do it at home in Game 5.

"Just keep doing what we're doing. Obviously we know what's at stake," Penguins captain Sidney Crosby said.

The Sharks were unable to build on their first win in the final, allowing the first goal for the fourth straight game and going more than nine minutes without a shot on goal during one stretch of the second period.

San Jose has yet to lead at any point in the series other than after scoring in overtime in Game 3.

"We've been chasing the game the whole series by not scoring first," coach Peter DeBoer said. "We have to find a way to get on the board earlier in the game instead of chasing it all night."

Melker Karlsson scored the lone goal and Martin Jones made 17 saves for San Jose.

No team has come back from a 3-1 deficit to win the final since Toronto did it in 1942 against Detroit.

The story for the Penguins after their 3-2 overtime loss in Game 3 was how to get Malkin going after a slow start to the series. And how would the rookie Murray respond after giving up the soft goal to Ward and the winner to Joonas Donskoi.

Both passed with flying colors.

Malkin was energized from the start, helping setting up the first goal when he caught San Jose on a bad line change and sent Phil Kessel in on a rush. Jones stopped Kessel's shot, but Cole knocked in the rebound for his first career playoff goal.

Malkin then got his goal when he tapped in a perfect from Kessel for Pittsburgh's first power-play goal of the series.

"I didn't change my game a lot," Malkin said. "I wanted a little bit more to play with the puck."

Murray wasn't tested often early and went nearly the first half of the second period without facing a single shot.

"I'm just trying to have fun through all of this," Murray said. "It's been an absolute blast so far. I'm going to look to keep that same mindset going forward."

The Sharks made a strong late push, and he robbed Couture, left all alone in the slot after a turnover by Kris Letang, late in the second.

Murray then stopped Patrick Marleau on a breakaway and saved a one-timer by Joe Pavelski early in the third before allowing his first goal. Karlsson beat him on a rebound of Brenden Dillon's point shot with 11:53 to play.

But Murray didn't flinch and came up big again against Pavelski, keeping the NHL's leading goal scorer this postseason without a point in the final.

"He's just been great," Crosby said. "He's just showing a lot of poise now, a lot of maturity."

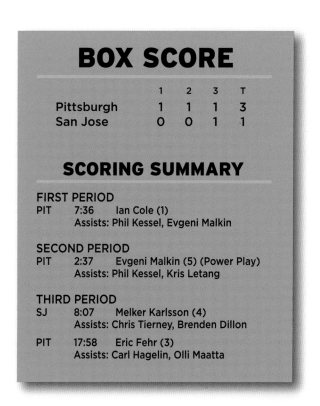

BOX SCORE

	1	2	3	T
Pittsburgh	1	1	1	3
San Jose	0	0	1	1

SCORING SUMMARY

FIRST PERIOD
PIT   7:36   Ian Cole (1)
           Assists: Phil Kessel, Evgeni Malkin

SECOND PERIOD
PIT   2:37   Evgeni Malkin (5) (Power Play)
           Assists: Phil Kessel, Kris Letang

THIRD PERIOD
SJ   8:07   Melker Karlsson (4)
           Assists: Chris Tierney, Brenden Dillon

PIT   17:58   Eric Fehr (3)
           Assists: Carl Hagelin, Olli Maatta

Penguins Bryan Rust, gives Sharks goalie Martin Jones a snow shower as he rushes the net. AP Photo

The Sharks Chris Tierney (50) checks the Penguins Patric Hornvist (72) over Sharks goalie Martin Jones (31). (AP Photo

STANLEY CUP FINALS

JUNE 9, 2016 CONSOL ENERGY CENTER PITTSBURGH, PENNSYLVANIA

PITTSBURGH PENGUINS 2 ● SAN JOSE SHARKS 4

JONES KEEPS SHARKS AFLOAT

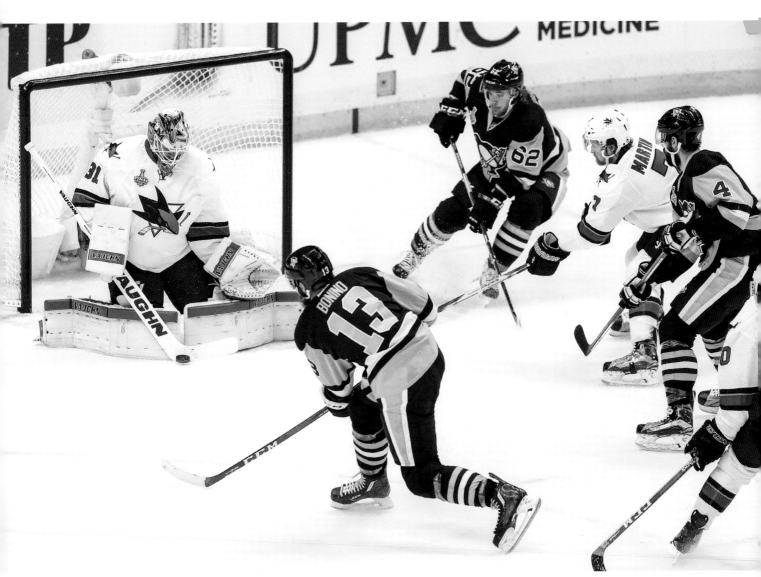

San Jose goalie Martin Jone (31) makes a save on a shot by Penguins center Nick Bonino (13) as teammate Carl Hagelin (62) looks for the rebound. AP Photo

San Jose Sharks goaltender Martin Jones is always looking to deflect attention elsewhere.

On this night, he couldn't stay out of the spotlight.

The Sharks and Penguins are heading back west for Game 6 after Jones turned aside 44 shots in a 4-2 victory in Game 5.

The Penguins Carl Hagelin (62) slips one past San Jose goalie Martin Jones (31) during the first period. **AP Photo**

Outplayed but not outscored, San Jose heads home with a chance to even the best-of-seven series at 3-3.

"Joner bailed us out tonight," said San Jose defenseman Justin Braun.

Repeatedly. The Sharks' breakthrough season on the line after they spent the better part of four games chasing -- but not quite catching -- relentless Pittsburgh, they responded by jumping on Penguins rookie goaltender Matt Murray early and then relying on Jones late.

Not that he wanted to talk about it, not even after becoming the first goaltender in the expansion era to win two games in the Stanley Cup finals while making at least 40 saves.

"I don't know, I felt good tonight," Jones said. "I thought our [defense] did a good job in front of the net and we got a few bounces tonight."

The Sharks, particularly their stars, gave him enough in the first period, and Jones had all the wiggle room he would need.

Logan Couture had a goal and two assists while Brent Burns, Melker Karlsson and captain Joe Pavelski also scored for San Jose, which was outshot 46-22 but held firm after surviving a chaotic opening five minutes and playing capably after getting the lead in regulation for the first time in the series.

"We know we haven't scored many goals in this series, and it's one of the reasons we're down 3-1," Couture said, "[but] we didn't want our season to end."

Evgeni Malkin and Carl Hagelin scored for Pittsburgh, but the 22-year-old Murray, whose postseason play helped fuel the Penguins' return to the finals after a seven-year break, faltered early, and his high-profile teammates struggled to get the puck by Jones.

"We were right there," Crosby said. "We hit a few posts. We were in around the net. Guys were working hard."

Just not enough to finish off the Sharks.

The Penguins stressed that the final step in the long slog from the tumult of December -- when Mike Johnston was fired and replaced with Mike Sullivan with the team languishing on the fringe of the playoff picture -- would be the most

difficult. Yet the prospect of celebrating the first title captured within the city limits in 56 years sent thousands into the streets around Consol Energy Center, and tickets were going for well over $1,000.

It took all of 64 seconds for the Sharks to quiet them and 2:53 to leave them stunned. Burns' first goal of the finals, a wrist shot from the circle that didn't look unlike Joonas Donskoi's overtime winner in Game 3, put San Jose in front in regulation for the first time in the series. Couture doubled San Jose's advantage less than two minutes later with a redirect in front of the net.

The momentum evaporated quickly. Malkin scored on the power play 4:44 into the first, and Hagelin followed 22 seconds later to tie it, the fastest opening four-goal sequence in the history of the finals.

Things settled down -- at least a little -- until Karlsson's shot from in front with just less than five minutes left in the first, set up by a pretty backhand feed from Couture.

"We played the way we needed to win the game," Murray said. "But their goalie stood on his head."

BOX SCORE

	1	2	3	T
Pittsburgh	2	0	0	2
San Jose	3	0	1	4

SCORING SUMMARY

FIRST PERIOD

SJ   1:04   Brent Burns (7)
Assists: Melker Karlsson, Logan Couture

SJ   2:53   Logan Couture (9)
Assist: Justin Braun

PIT   4:44   Evgeni Malkin (6) (Power Play)
Assists: Phil Kessel, Kris Letang

PIT   5:06   Carl Hagelin (6)
Assist: Nick Bonino

SJ   14:47   Melker Karlsson (5)
Assists: Logan Couture, Brenden Dillon

THIRD PERIOD

SJ   18:40   Joe Pavelski (14)
Assist: Joe Thornton

Penguins players rush onto the ice and celebrate after winning the Stanley Cup. AP Photo

STANLEY CUP FINALS

JUNE 12, 2016 SAP CENTER SAN JOSE, CALIFORNIA

PITTSBURGH PENGUINS 3 • SAN JOSE SHARKS 1

PENGUINS WIN FOURTH STANLEY CUP

Teammates congratulate defenseman Brian Dumoulin (8) after his first period goal put the Penguins up 1-0. AP Photo

Sidney Crosby let out a scream as he lifted the Stanley Cup above his head, a wide smile spread across his face.

The seven years of adversity since he last held the trophy were firmly in his past. The concussions that nearly derailed his career. The early playoff exits. The rough start to this season that led to a coach being fired.

Penguins goalie Matt Murray (30) makes a huge save on a shot by Sharks right winger Joonas Donskoi during the second period.   AP Photo

Penguins center Nick Bonino (13) shoots a backhand shot as Sharks Patrick Marleau (12) and goalie Martin Jones (31) defend during the third period. **AP Photo**

Crosby and the Penguins are once again champions.

A kid no more and surrounded with new talent, Crosby set up Kris Letang's go-ahead goal midway through the second period and Pittsburgh won the fourth Stanley Cup in franchise history by beating the San Jose Sharks 3-1 in Game 6. Owner Mario Lemieux thrust his hands into the air in triumph high up in an arena suite and later hugged his superstar on the ice.

This title had been a long time coming.

"I was just thinking about how hard it was to get to this point, just trying to enjoy every second of it," Crosby said. "It's not easy to get here. Having won seven years ago at a young age, you probably take it for granted a little bit. You don't think you do at the time, but it's not easy to get to this point."

Brian Dumoulin opened the scoring with a power-play goal and Patric Hornqvist added a late empty-netter. Matt Murray made 18 saves to give the Penguins a championship seven years to the day after they beat Detroit for their third title. The game ended when Crosby cleared the puck the length of the ice with San Jose on the power play, setting off a wild celebration.

All that was left was for Crosby to accept the Conn Smythe trophy as playoff MVP and then the Stanley Cup.

"He's a special player for a reason," teammate Chris Kunitz said. "He can adapt and change his game to different things. Early in his career he went out and got points and did everything but that didn't make him satisfied. He had to go out and lead through example and became a better player."

Three nights after squandering a chance to become the first Pittsburgh team to win a title in front of the home fans in 56 years, the Penguins finished the job on the road just like they did in Minnesota (1991), Chicago (1992) and Detroit (2009) in past title runs.

The championship in Detroit was supposed to be the first of many for a team led by players like Crosby and Evgeni Malkin. But a series of concussions cost Crosby almost an entire season and a half, and there were those playoff disappointments that included twice blowing 3-1 series leads. There was no second celebration in the Crosby era -- until now.

This didn't seem like it would be a season to remember back in early December when the Penguins were the near the bottom of the standings in the Eastern Conference and coach Mike Johnston was fired.

But led by coach Mike Sullivan, the Penguins recovered to make the playoffs as the second-place team in the Metropolitan Division after some shrewd moves by general manager Jim Rutherford, who put together the entire "HBK line" of Carl Hagelin, Nick Bonino and Phil Kessel over the past year as well as other key acquisitions.

Pittsburgh knocked off the New York Rangers in the first round, Presidents' Trophy-winning Washington in round two and then rallied from a 3-2 series deficit to beat Tampa Bay in the Eastern Conference final.

"In the playoffs, suddenly we thought we could beat any team," Malkin said. "We tried to play the same game we played in 2009."

The Penguins were in control for almost the entire final. They did not trail until Game 5 at home and responded to a strong push from San Jose in the clincher to avoid a decisive seventh game. Pittsburgh held San Jose to just one shot on goal in the first 19 minutes of the third period to preserve the one-goal lead. The Penguins sealed it when Crosby blocked a shot from Marc-Edouard Vlasic that set up Hornqvist's empty-netter.

"You dream your whole life for this," said Kessel, the former Maple Leaf who led the Penguins with 22 points this postseason. "How can you ask for anything better than this? Winning the Cup is what you dream of and what you play for."

Logan Couture scored the lone goal for the Sharks, who were making their first trip to the final in their 25-year history. Martin Jones made 24 saves and was San Jose's best player for the series.

There was an electric atmosphere before the final home game of the season in San Jose with fans starting their "Let's Go Sharks!" chants well before the opening puck. But the Penguins jumped ahead for the fifth time in six games this series after Dainius Zubrus was sent off for tripping when Crosby's line didn't allow San Jose to leave its own zone. Dumoulin took advantage when his point shot beat Jones for a rare soft goal allowed by the Sharks' netminder.

The Sharks tied it early in the period when Couture beat Murray with a big shot for his 30th point of the postseason. Pittsburgh answered 1:19 later when Crosby sent a pass from behind the net to Letang, who beat Jones from a sharp angle to the short side to make it 2-1.

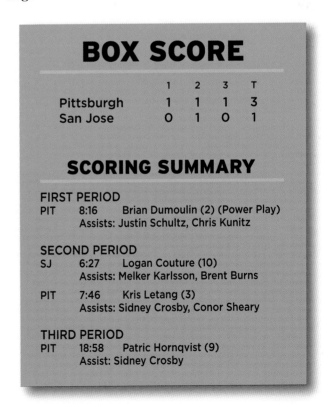

BOX SCORE

	1	2	3	T
Pittsburgh	1	1	1	3
San Jose	0	1	0	1

SCORING SUMMARY

FIRST PERIOD
PIT   8:16   Brian Dumoulin (2) (Power Play)
Assists: Justin Schultz, Chris Kunitz

SECOND PERIOD
SJ   6:27   Logan Couture (10)
Assists: Melker Karlsson, Brent Burns

PIT   7:46   Kris Letang (3)
Assists: Sidney Crosby, Conor Sheary

THIRD PERIOD
PIT   18:58   Patric Hornqvist (9)
Assist: Sidney Crosby

Below: Kris Letang (58) and Carl Hagelin (62) celebrate a Stanley Cup championship. AP Photo

Above: Penguins owner Mario Lemieux congratulates captain Sidney Crosby. AP Photo

PENGUINS ROSTER

CENTERS

NO.	NAME	AGE	HT	WT	SHOT	BIRTH PLACE	BIRTHDATE
13	Nick Bonino	28	6-1	194	L	Hartford, Connecticut	4/20/88
87	Sidney Crosby	28	5-11	200	L	Cole Harbour, Nova Scotia	8/7/87
7	Matt Cullen	39	6-0	200	L	Virginia, Minnesota	11/2/76
39	Jean-Sabastien Dea	22	5-11	175	R	Laval, Quebec	2/8/94
71	Evgeni Malkin	29	6-3	212	L	Magnitogorsk, USSR	7/31/86
22	Kael Mouillierat	28	6-0	188	L	Edmonton, Alberta	9/9/87
11	Kevin Porter	30	5-11	191	L	Detroit, Michigan	3/12/86
49	Dominik Simon	21	5-11	176	L	Prague, Czech Republic	8/8/94
40	Oskar Sundqvist	22	6-3	209	R	Boden, Sweden	3/23/94
23	Scott Wilson	24	5-11	183	L	Oakville, Ontario	4/24/92

LEFT WINGS

NO.	NAME	AGE	HT	WT	SHOT	BIRTH PLACE	BIRTHDATE
62	Carl Hagelin	27	6-0	186	L	Sodertalje, Sweden	8/23/88
14	Chris Kunitz	36	6-0	193	L	Regina, Saskatchewan	9/26/79
47	Tom Sestito	28	6-5	228	L	Utica, New York	9/28/87
43	Conor Sheary	23	5-9	175	L	Winchester, Massachusetts	6/8/92

RIGHT WINGS

NO.	NAME	AGE	HT	WT	SHOT	BIRTH PLACE	BIRTHDATE
45	Josh Archibald	23	5-10	176	R	Regina, Saskatchewan	10/6/92
19	Beau Bennett	24	6-1	190	R	Gardena, California	11/27/91
16	Eric Fehr	30	6-4	212	R	Winkler, Manitoba	9/7/85
72	Patric Hornqvist	29	5-11	189	R	Sollentuna, Sweden	1/1/87
81	Phil Kessel	28	6-0	202	R	Madison, Wisconsin	10/2/87
34	Tom Kuhnhackl	24	6-2	196	L	Landshut, Germany	1/21/92
17	Bryan Rust	24	5-11	192	R	Pontiac, Michigan	5/11/92
41	Daniel Sprong	19	6-0	180	R	Amsterdam, Netherlands	3/17/97

DEFENSE

NO.	NAME	AGE	HT	WT	SHOT	BIRTH PLACE	BIRTHDATE
28	Ian Cole	27	6-1	219	L	Ann Arbor, Michigan	2/21/89
6	Trevor Daley	32	5-11	195	L	Toronto, Ontario	10/9/83
8	Brian Dumoulin	24	6-4	207	L	Biddeford, Maine	9/6/91
44	Tim Erixon	26	6-2	190	L	Port Chester, New York	2/24/90
58	Kris Letang	29	6-0	200	R	Montreal, Quebec	4/24/87
12	Ben Lovejoy	32	6-2	215	R	Concord, New Hampshire	2/20/84
3	Olli Maatta	21	6-1	204	L	Jyvaskyla, Finland	8/22/94
65	Steven Oleksy	30	6-0	190	R	Chesterfield, Michigan	2/4/86
51	Derrick Pouliot	22	5-11	195	L	Estevan, Saskatchewan	1/16/94
4	Justin Schultz	25	6-2	196	R	Kelowna, British Columbia	7/6/90

GOALIES

NO.	NAME	AGE	HT	WT	SHOT	BIRTH PLACE	BIRTHDATE
29	Marc-Andre Fleury	31	6-2	185	L	Sorel, Quebec	11/28/84
35	Tristan Jarry	21	6-2	194	L	Surrey, British Columbia	4/29/95
30	Matt Murray	22	6-4	178	L	Thunder Bay, Ontario	5/25/94
37	Jeff Zatkoff	28	6-1	179	L	Detroit, Michigan	6/9/87